I'M IN LOVE
WITH A
MARRIED MAN

I'M IN LOVE
WITH A
MARRIED MAN

H. S. Vigeveno

A. J. HOLMAN COMPANY · 1976

Division of J. B. Lippincott Company

Philadelphia and New York

U.S. Library of Congress Cataloging in Publication Data

Vigeveno, H   S
    I'm in love with a married man.

    1. Adultery—Case studies. 2. Women—Religious
life—Case studies. I. Title.
HQ806.V53   261.8′34′153   76-22495
ISBN–0–87981–067–X

Contents

Introduction   7

1. Four Personal Stories   11

2. Getting Over an Emotional Involvement:
    A Correspondence   78

3. Needs and Desires   90

4. Counseling the Woman in Love:
    An Interview with Dr. John C. Mebane   99

5. From Conflict to Resolution:
    Finding the Way   112

Introduction

I supremo it's the most difficult problem I've faced. That's why I asked several women to talk about their affairs with married men. It was a challenge for me not only to explore this problem but also to find some answers!

I have witnessed the splitting up of too many families where the one factor, *the one decisive factor*, was another man (or woman). Statistics could probably reveal that falling in love with someone has been at the root of many a divorce action, perhaps more than any other single cause.

And it's a *tough* problem. As difficult as it is to overcome a physical addiction like alcoholism or gluttony, it is even more difficult to battle an emotional one. Perhaps that's what we should label this falling in love with a married man—an emotional addiction. It is no light matter that can be dismissed overnight, and for the person who holds high morals this issue is compounded.

I am not concerned in this book about casual attachments which raise little if any ethical qualms. The lovely French actress Catherine Deneuve was quoted as having said: "I have absolutely no regret and no shame regarding any relationship I have ever had with any man." *

Our drama, however, takes place because people with spiritual roots are wrestling with their conscience. Their faith hangs in the balance. Christians who believe that God has said, "Thou shalt not commit adultery," † and who have at first hesitantly and then deliberately—and sometimes repeatedly—broken this command are caught up in a great crisis. How they resolve their dilemmas is not only of great interest but one of the main reasons for writing this book.

I have interviewed these women with the use of a tape recorder, so that their original stories are told in their own words. Every woman read and approved her chapter before it was put into print. Sufficient details have been changed to hide their identities; thus, the temptation to identify persons should be resisted. These stories took place in *four* different denominations and *five* different congregations, so they cannot be traced to any one congregation I have served.

"Why are there no interviews with men?" you may wonder. There could very well have been, but I have focused on the more emotional attachments of the women. Most men are more interested in the sexual aspects of a relationship, and to explore these would lead to another book!

I am indebted to these women who were not afraid to expose their emotions by way of personal testimony; and to all who find themselves in a similar conflict—a conflict of the emotions, the will, and the heart—this book is sincerely dedicated.

* As quoted in *Time* magazine.
† Exodus 20:14.

*I feel the more I know God
that He would sooner we did wrong in loving,
than never love
for fear we should do wrong.*

From *The Life and Letters of Father Andrew*

1
Four Personal Stories

No. 1

"I DON'T KNOW of a working woman, no matter what her religious background is, who isn't at one time or another involved with a married man! If they are divorced women, they have the time at their disposal, but even married women are getting involved. I mean, I'm not naïve to the business. They don't always tell their stories, but even if they have to work things in at strange times, like lunchtime, or go shopping with the women, it's not really shopping with the women! The joke is, you have to call around and ask a friend to say 'I went shopping with you last night,' in case your husband wants to know your whereabouts."

We were waiting for our dinner in a fashionable restaurant as she told me her story. She would occasionally lapse into these generalizations. She was very bright and quick of mind. Nothing escaped her. She was also very beautiful, and not a few had turned their heads as we were seated at our table. She was certainly conscious of the attention, although she had trouble accepting it. A charming woman with a captivating smile, I thought as I questioned her about falling in love with a married man. Five years after her divorce it had happened. She had been single then. Prior to that time she had been careful to avoid married men, since she had a deep faith and was active in the church. Besides, her divorce had torn her apart emotionally.

"How did this relationship start?" I asked.

"Well, I was single and available," she replied. "I met him at work. We had a common interest. I find this is where it often happens. I've talked with a number of women and that's usually the story. He made me feel he needed me, my companionship."

"You work in an office and you sensed that he needed you as a person?" I continued.

"Yes. A married man who is not happy at home, who finds that his wife doesn't understand his work, needs someone who will understand. I understood him. Listened to him. He told me about his unhappiness at home. And a wife who is raising small children is tired. Besides, *he* is tired of having baby talk to come home to."

"So it starts off with business talk."

"Yes. And a rapport starts building. Some people say it is clandestine excitement. I don't know—it may be. But he was a very brilliant person and I had the top secretarial job. We both felt important to each other. I felt important because I had his attention."

"How did your relationship develop then?"

"It started with a few lunches, then dinners, then going places together."

"And all the time you knew that he was married?"

"I did. He was going through the I'm-unhappily-married-and-I'm-going-to-get-a-divorce bit. And I kind of built on that. *For years* I built on that! Eventually you say to him: 'I'm not going to see you anymore.' And he says, 'Give me a little more time because of the children.' And that's where it rests. So then you consider the children. For years you consider the children!"

"How long did this relationship continue?"

"About six years, off and on. Breaking off and starting up again. After the first year I said I was not going to see him again. I went through a lot of trauma. I moved, had my phone changed, that type of thing. I tried to get away from the situation and set everything right. But he came back with his sad stories—'I need you' and so on. And then, well, a woman often threatens but she doesn't mean it. Even in marriage. We use scare tactics, and all the time we want to feel loved and needed. He would bounce back into my life and I never quite got over it. He would call once in a while, as he does now."

"He is still calling you?"

"Occasionally, yes. But I'm not in love with him anymore. I'm in love with someone else, someone who's eligible. The married man with whom I was in love says that he's still in love with me, but it's never worked out."

"You mean he promised to leave his wife and never did?"

"And never will," she said quickly. "They've even talked about it, so he says. But he has a hang-up with the children. Besides, a man finds it very difficult to admit failure. And that's what it would be for him with his background, trying to live up to his father's demands. He can't afford to fail."

"You really believe that he was in love with you?"

"As much as he was capable of loving. He has another affair going now. And he openly went with someone else when we broke up, but he says it's still me. But what is that?"

"Even after he went with the other woman you still retained your feelings for him?"

She let the word spit through her teeth: "Sick!" she said. "Believe me, I didn't want to. It's totally inexplainable. And even though I wanted to end the relationship, I went back into it. And every time it would leave me shattered."

We were being served our salad while we talked, and surrounding us like a curtain was the clatter of dishes and voices from other tables.

"You must have been in a lot of turmoil while this affair was going on," I commented. "What created this conflict of feelings within you?"

"I think, for one thing, I wanted to hold up my head in society. I wanted to be accepted along with him, to have holidays and birthdays together, but obviously we couldn't. We did have some weekends together, but it was always a frightening experience if someone would see us." She poked at her salad. "I didn't like living this way. I've always been able to do things right, and there was the religious feeling, too. I knew the relationship could never be blessed."

"How did he get away from his wife on weekends?"

"He'd say he was going out of town on business. She was gullible enough to accept it. He made excuses during the week for his late nights. Perhaps she didn't want to know the truth."

"But it bothered you," I reiterated.

"Yes. It was an ego thing. No matter how much he would say he loved me, he always went home to her! She was still holding the winning cards, and I couldn't stand it."

"How would you have felt if he had broken up his family for you?"

She thought for a moment, had another bite and said: "Well, he was a lousy father. And their relationship was dead. I thought there was nothing between them. So I rationalized that she would have a decent life."

"But you wouldn't feel conscience stricken, let's say, if you had been successful with him?"

"No. In that particular situation I would not have. But that is an unusual case. His children didn't even know him, because he was never home. She was living in misery and she could have had a decent life without him. There was anger and no talking—so much unhappiness between them. But I think that if a man does leave his wife for you, you go through a certain amount of pain for that wife and the children. You can't put that family back together again. And if he leaves the children, he will never forget them. Not really."

She was silent for a moment. Then she added: "I wonder if it is ever possible that another woman breaks up a marriage? If the marriage is strong enough, would the husband let the woman 'break up' that marriage?"

I admitted that it was a good question. And yet how many times had an affair become the reason for a husband's or a wife's taking the fatal step? We returned to the problem of guilt.

"I would also say that the other woman—me," she

continued, "would have a feeling of great jubilation because the man cared that much for her. Of course, I would carry a certain amount of guilt. Especially because of the effect on the children. Even if we left the state, as some men do, to start over again, you can't really forget it. It's something within you."

We were served dinner, and we paused to make some small talk and started eating.

"When you get to a certain age," she continued, "there isn't anyone running about who is available, single, thirty plus, and attractive. The ones who are available you have nothing in common with, you know. Who would want them anyway? So the question becomes whether you'd rather be alone or with someone."

While she continued to eat I switched the conversation a bit: "You were brought up very religiously?"

"Very."

"A strong faith?"

"Yes."

"It had always been a part of your life?"

"True."

"You never turned against God in bitterness, or denied your faith?"

"No."

"But what did it do to you when you went against your moral code?"

"That was very difficult for me. Each morning I would get on my knees and confess what I had done or who I had been with the night before and ask for forgiveness. But I was really so happy with that person that I would not give him up. And I had this conflict going the entire time. Now it is very easy for someone to say

I should give him up and another would come along, but that's simply not true."

What she was saying was that you cannot make substitutions with persons. Each one is an individual. You cannot replace one affair with another. Those who attempt it eventually lose the spark of love, as well as a sense of the value of persons.

"Some ministers will say that a single person should do without sex," she commented. "That is my bone of contention with them. Most of my friends are in their thirties and divorced. I've talked the subject over with them. They don't agree with those who say that men are human and need sex but women don't. I've gone through all that abstinence and sleepless nights. I don't do that anymore. I've had sex and I don't feel condemned. God does not condemn me, but I do have a conscience and I set controls." She stopped a moment. "If you care for someone and love someone, isn't that what counts?"

I allowed the question to hang.

"Besides, if you're going to follow the rules, by my divorce I had already messed it up."

" 'Whom God has joined together let no man put asunder,' " I quoted.

"Yes. You've already messed that up. You see, I believe a woman is a human being too. She has the same functions. And I refuse to live on Miltown for the rest of my life. I went that route too long. Suffering? Nightmares? The doctors were telling me that I shouldn't be going through all that. So I gave myself to him, completely and totally."

She told me that their relations were the best she

had ever experienced. We would return to the subject later, but at this time I kept on questioning her about the conflict: "When you failed to get him to leave his family for you, did this precipitate a crisis?"

"Yes, definitely. We believed that our love was so special, so right. I believed that very much. It felt so right. And I took it personally that the failure was in me. Why wouldn't he leave her and marry me? And I suffered. Oh, I suffered beautifully for over a year or so. And everyone knew I suffered. I felt I could not love anyone else, ever. Then I cursed God for that pain. I asked why. I asked God daily, I begged him. And I would go through a whole day of prayer, asking like that. I suffered better than anyone I know!"

"To punish yourself?"

"I guess so. I was pleading for God to send an answer. To cure this heartache. And before that I had never been able to understand women in love."

She smiled at me and then started to eat again.

"You mean that in your marriage you didn't have quite the same feelings that you experienced for this married man?"

"No—no comparison. Unfortunately."

"This was really the first love of your life?"

"*The* love, yes. I've been in love before, but when it was over I put myself together and did something else. Not this time. Nothing helped me at all."

"So this was really something special?"

"Yes, yes, it was. Even now when he calls me I should hang up, but I don't. And I can't really tell the man whom I presently love. He gets very jealous. He comes by my desk and says, 'Who are you talking to on the phone?' Once I wrote the name on a piece of paper, and he went crazy. So I don't do that anymore."

She laughed. "You know," she said, "my perfectly honest relationship with the man I now love went down the tubes! We thought we could share everything. As to the man I loved, he is completely selfish. I didn't know that before. I understand it now. I told him that I've found someone else, and I'm happy. He says he can't stand that, so he still calls me. We shared so much in years past, almost everything. I know how he thinks, and he knows me too."

"But there's nothing beyond the telephone conversations now?"

"No, I wouldn't allow that."

"So you are the one who has the strength to call a halt."

"Oh, yes. I can't gain anything from it."

"How did you arrive at that place finally?"

There was a long pause. She had to think about it a while: this was the heart of the matter. Then she spoke two words very slowly: "Time and love." I asked her to explain.

"After so much time and so many other dates there was still no one like him. But what it did was to put some time between. It lessened the pain. Now there is someone else and love. It's been a long time coming. I didn't believe it could ever happen, but it has. Time and love," she repeated.

We found ourselves eating occasionally, although the food was getting colder. We talked again about the triangle.

"I suppose," she philosophized, "that most women

would not really want to know whether their husband was seeing another woman, because that would mean that *they* had failed. And no person likes to admit failure. Perhaps some look for failure because of their insecurity. But you don't want to admit that you have failed because it means you have to change something! To grow, to listen, to change your way of life. We're secure where we are in our little ruts. And this girl," she pointed to herself as she spoke, "thought she was worthless, so she didn't believe she could have anyone else. She stayed in that unhappy, uncommunicative situation because that was all she felt worthy of."

"Was he a handsome man?"

"Yes, but in a conservative kind of way. Not the type I would usually fall for. Tall. Dynamic. But it all depends on what your needs are. You fall for someone who fulfills your needs and builds your ego."

"You didn't fall in love with his looks, then?"

"Not really. In fact, I changed his dress style. Changed his appearance. Got him into a bigger car."

"But he was attracted to your looks?"

She couldn't quite say yes to that, in spite of her striking appearance.

"He was attracted to my *happy*," she said. "I laughed a lot. He needed that gaiety."

I persisted: "Didn't you think he was attracted to your looks, too?"

"Well—I never thought about it at the time. Probably." She laughed again a bit nervously. "You know, I never thought I was an attractive woman. But after counseling I found out some of the causes. One reason why I didn't think I was attractive was due to the fact that I could never figure out why my real father left me. Subconsciously, I blamed myself. I know now how wrong that was. He didn't leave because of me but for many other reasons. I was only three at the time. I remember I used to call myself an ugly, fat baby. I never could look at my baby pictures, not until recently. And then I had a stepfather who resented me because I was another man's child. He ignored me, my entire life! I would come into a room loud—to gain his attention—and he would get up and walk out. I would become more boisterous, because some emotion is better than none. I have gone through all my life being loud, wanting people to notice me."

She spoke very quietly in measured tones. But in a group, I knew, she emanated a vivaciousness that attracted attention. Now she understood why she had been like that—had behaved like that, in fact, since childhood.

"I never wanted anyone to dislike me. So after I failed with this married man, I faced a real crisis. I went to charm school. I'm in my thirties and I was totally devastated, insecure. I wanted them to tell me what was wrong with me."

"To improve your looks?"

"Perhaps, but also to find out why I couldn't hold his love, when it seemed so right. I had failed again. I had given everything and lost! It's taken me a while to realize I'm not ugly. Now, when people give me compliments, I try to accept them. They really mean it. But I was self-conscious and emphasized my ugly features to myself. I thought people were saying 'You're beautiful' because they were trying to be nice. Now I check all the positives. I have to work at my weight and I'm not ashamed of my age anymore."

When she stated her age I had to admit that she didn't look it. I had guessed her to be about ten years younger, and I usually don't miss by that much. I didn't, however, think she had a weight problem; it had been built up in her own mind. Following the affair, she had come to a better understanding of herself through counseling. She began to feel some worth as a person. She knew who she was.

So I continued: "Since you didn't have a good self-image, you were flattered by the attentions of men. Was this perhaps one of the reasons why you became involved with a married man?"

"Yes. And I have learned something else. Subconsciously, and I didn't know this at the time, I *wanted* to get involved with someone I couldn't have. That would result in another put-down. I deserved that, you see. That's why I gave so much to this married man."

"But since you have become aware of all this, hasn't it thrown your affair into a different light?"

"Yes." Again she stopped, took a deep breath, and then added: "You see, a woman thinks with her heart."

"I know. Your feelings. But at least you understand things a little better."

"Yes, and I'm not afraid. People have seen the difference in my job. I used to hang back, but now I speak up. I can even stand up to the top boss. Before you can be assertive you have to believe in yourself."

She was telling me happily of her newly found freedom. "Some women keep the same patterns. They stay married to the same man, even though they are unhappy. Some single women keep going from one married man to another, all because of this self-image thing."

"But you think you have broken it?"

"Oh yes." She was very positive. "It is a sweet-and-sour situation with a married man. I have known kept women. The husband will never leave his wife. So he keeps the other woman, maybe even sets her up in an apartment, or a house. How many women go to counselors to understand themselves? To get real help? And sometimes, when they begin with a counselor, he'll make a pass at her or say, 'Go to bed with everyone.' That *destroys* the self-image. It just sets a woman further back."

"Suppose," I asked, "you had come to me in the midst of this affair and you knew it was wrong and wanted to get over it, but you didn't have the willpower. How could I have helped you?"

"In the first place, you don't talk a woman out of something. If you had told me, 'Give him up,' I would never have come back. You have to deal first with why I got into it, to uncover my needs. And then you have to talk to me about myself, to find out what my background is. It all comes back to that self-image. That's the way to go, but even then it will be a difficult thing. If you're talking to a woman of thirty-five or forty, she's not going to find someone else so easily. And you're dealing with her emotions, not just her logic. A woman thinks with her feelings, and that's how she falls back into an affair. It offers security and love."

I shared with her the fact that I face such counseling situations where insight is not enough and even prayer sticks in the throat. She continued:

23

"You can't replace love unless you have love. There's no way you can tell a woman that the closeness, the warmth, the love from someone who cares for her is not important. When I'm home by myself that doesn't work itself out. Alone is alone is *alone*. . . . I've been there."

"Where does faith enter in here? What about God?"

"That's where most people have a lot of trouble. They turn their backs on God because the married man is filling a warmth right that minute, and they don't feel God present like that. That's what the church should deal with. Besides when people are divorced, they often walk out on God because they have failed him. Then they leave themselves wide open. It's just not enough to say God is with you, when you want human warmth and love too."

We were served more coffee and I allowed her to finish eating, while I continued to probe: "When a woman of forty, let's say, gains insight into herself, and she wants to get away from this particular involvement but there is no one else, how does she cope? What else did you do?"

"I'm not forty yet. O.K. Soon, but not yet. You keep moving. You make friends. You don't stay home alone. You surround yourself with people. That's what I did, but it's taken me five years to get over it. You can't stop living. I went to church too. But it doesn't take the place."

It had been a tough struggle for her. Even as she pulled away from him, he was continually in her thoughts. Day in and day out: "I thought about him constantly."

"But you didn't go back with him."

"No. I couldn't. I knew it would be the same thing all over again."

"You were *constantly* thinking about him?"

"Yes. I never met anyone better. I wouldn't allow myself to."

"In spite of this preoccupation, you didn't pick up the phone and ask to see him?"

"That's right. *He* would call eventually."

"And then?"

"I didn't go back if that's what you mean."

"Even though you wanted to?"

She hesitated. "Once I faltered and decided to see him again. I knew he was temporarily separated from his wife. As we got back together he said, 'You're the one person who makes me happy.' It lasted for three times and then he was back home. 'Because of the children,' he told me. That shattered me. I almost wanted to destroy myself. One more rejection and I thought I'd have an emotional breakdown."

She took a deep breath. "You see, our sexual bond was a very strong one. For the first time in my life I was really happy, satisfied. I felt like a real woman. Since that was gone too I tried to become very celibate." She switched again. "Now, in my recent conversations with him, I realize I have a very strong affection for him, but I don't love him anymore. Not like I used to. He hasn't changed, but I am able to control my own feelings."

I listened patiently. She continued on the subject.

"I know three other women who are all Christians with similar problems. They had a point of pride where they split up, but the only thing that eventually changed

their lives was a new love. And it didn't happen overnight. I wish I could say, along with Women's Libera-
tion, that I think we're equal to men, but woman is not
an independent creature. She may be equal in a lot
of things, but we're very emotional and dependent."

I was about to wind up our conversation. "I must
admit," I said, "that when I first met you, you came
across as an outgoing, happy person—yet underneath I
noticed a hardness."

"Embittered—disillusioned—cynical." The words
were her own.

"But it's not there any longer."

"No, it's gone. Because of counseling, insight, love.
Still, I can understand the cynics. They're hurt, confused. They have that love-is-always-going-to-go-wrong
kind of feeling. Of course, when I experienced rejection
because this married man would not get a divorce, it
followed the pattern of my father leaving mother (and
me), my uncommunicative stepfather, and my divorce.
Perhaps other men. Now I have loved and lost. It reinforced my bitterness, and then I reasoned with myself—
that's where they all end up. That's the way men are. It's
frightening that, after you have many rejections, you
don't want to try again. You don't want to pile up any
more failures."

We had a final cup of coffee. She was willing to
share more:

"The church will always have married groups, but
no one seems to take a look at these problems. Each
person who gets involved in some affair thinks she is the
only one. Then she feels ashamed and ostracized and
doesn't talk to anybody. Even when she goes to church
she can't get into the swing of it, because she feels she

has done wrong and there is no one to talk to about it. She's not living up to the rules. Now I see God in a different way. The God I feared before is not a God of just rules. I have a good relationship with God as love. I have come to understand that Jesus has already suffered tremendously for my sins. Why should I suffer too? That doesn't mean I'm going rampantly to go out and commit adultery and all that. But he understands the anguish I went through, the despair. I keep on my knees every morning because it is a learning process for me. Now the way I think, the love of my God explodes inside of me all the time. Before I feared him, I was angry with him, but now he's not way off there in the distance, but personal."

"Did you ever share your Christian faith with this married man?"

"Yes, we did some things together. He's a believer too, but now he doesn't practice it."

"Does he blame you for that?"

"I guess it's an easy way out for him."

"But your relationship at the time didn't shatter the faith of either of you?"

"No. He said that anything as beautiful as our love God would understand. To him God was a God of love."

"But at that time you feared God?"

"Right. Feared and hated. I had a God of rules then. And I learned that I suffered so long because I thought that I *should* suffer that long."

She threw her head back and laughed heartily at herself. It was a release. We talked further about the insight she had gained. "It has just been a miracle to me. It has changed my entire life!" She had also discovered some tools to work with: "You start with new data into the computer. New data every day, and soon it gets to be much stronger."

She laughed again and with the music playing in the background we left the booth and walked out of the restaurant.

No. 2

"Sometimes I think, you know, how did I get into this in the first place? A wave kind of goes through me. And I ask myself, 'How could this happen to you?' Here I had a lovely home, a family, and everything was going quite right. O.K. So I'm not on top of the world all the time. Then all of a sudden everything is completely changed, like overnight. Now I find myself in an apartment without my husband—I thought that's what I wanted, to be free; but it isn't really. Sometimes it's kind of hard to accept."

I remembered the very day she moved into that apartment. She called me when it really hit her. She was in tears, utterly shook up because of the reality of a divorce in process after more than twenty years of married life. Now she served me coffee in that apartment as we talked together about the events which had precipitated the divorce.

She had a genuine kindness about her, a warmth and attractiveness. Her apartment was comfortably and tastefully fixed up. Her faith had always meant very much to her, and her personal problems had thrown her into an emotional turmoil. She could not understand herself and she had sought counseling to resolve those inner conflicts. In her church she was a leader, looked up to by the membership, as she proved herself very capable and gave of herself willingly to the kingdom of God.

"I was raised very strict in the church," she began. "We were denied more things than we were allowed to do. I remember Sundays especially. They were days when we were not allowed to read the funny papers or go to the store. No shopping at all. Sundays consisted of Sunday school and church. Then we'd come home and have lunch and take a nap."

I smiled a little.

"That's right," she said, "because we couldn't do anything else, play with our friends, listen to the radio, or anything. So we took a nap and then went back to church."

"And you accepted all that?"

"Yes, I accepted it. What else was there to do?"

"Did you ever rebel?"

"No, never." She shook her head. "It wouldn't have done any good. Even in my teens I stayed with it. I never considered anything else."

She spoke in a quiet, little girl–like voice. It seemed as if she put herself back into those simple years when life had boundaries and limits were clearly defined.

"When I was married it was in the church. Both my husband and I were members. Our parents belonged there and so did our grandparents. We were three generations deep."

"Were you in love with him when you married him?"

"I certainly thought so and I had high hopes for the marriage. But now—you know, it was just the thing to do at the time. We didn't have too many to choose from, and circumstances were such that this seemed right. I thought I was in love with him. I was pretty naïve, though. I just went along with the plans. Once they were made you sort of fall into them. I was too young, barely eighteen."

"And how did your marriage work out? Were you happy in the beginning?"

"I think it worked out fine for a while. I didn't think anything differently. Just everyday living. We were both working. I worked until we had our first child. We were both working at an insurance company, so we had something in common. After the children came I stopped working until they were in school. Then I started again."

"How did you meet this married man?"

"At church."

"He was a member there?"

"He joined some years back."

"Did he become as active as you were?"

"No, but he and his family did get involved."

"Were you physically attracted to him?"

"No, I don't think so. Not really at first. Although he is good-looking." She stopped to think for a moment. "I guess what started it was that he wanted to talk to me. He had heard some things through his wife (she's somewhat of a busybody), and he thought they were rather strange. So he asked if we could meet and have a talk."

"What do you mean by strange things?"

"Oh, about a mutual friend of ours in the congregation, and what they were saying. He couldn't understand it, so he wanted to see me about it. He thought I could clear it up, I guess."

"Why did he seek you out without your husband?"

She sat back for a moment, looked at me, shifted, and replied: "You know, that's a good question. I've never thought about it. Well, I guess some of the gossip pertained to me rather than to my husband."

"Were you at that time in your marriage disillusioned, or was it going pretty well?"

"I was disillusioned," she replied. "I was searching. I was aware that there were some things lacking in our relationship."

"What, if anything, bothered you the most in your marriage?"

Again she paused to think. She had some coffee and remained quiet for what seemed a long while. Then she pulled her legs under her to relax.

"We had been married almost fifteen years and there was no real closeness. No great affection. Nothing deep. It was all you-do-what-you-do-because-that's-what-you're-supposed-to-do or -feel or -think, and we just went through life like that. Working. Kids. School. Church. Our everyday pattern with no real depth to it. My husband didn't make me feel appreciated. I received no encouragement in most things I was trying to do. Sure, he was always helpful. Anything I'd ask him to do he would do, whether at church or at home. I appreciated that. But it was never with enthusiasm. He always made me feel that he had to do it but didn't want to. And never a word of 'You did a good job,' or commendation for me."

"But as far as religion was concerned you were in harmony there?"

"That's true. There were times we could pray together. He would lead family devotions, but then he would let up again. I felt good about our times of prayer when we had them."

She stopped again and then summarized her thoughts about her husband. "I lost respect for him. That was really the heart of the problem. My respect for him went down."

"How did you lose respect for him?" I wanted to know.

"He was very one way about things, very definite. What he thinks is right is right. He can only see things his way. He gets what he wants. He sometimes embarrasses me in front of others because of this. He wants them to know that he's right, and to prove a point he'll do it in public. I think some of that is so childish. I've probably matured more than he, and this bothers me too. There are times when he just plain bores me."

"When you met with this married man the first time, did you already have romantic thoughts about him?"

"No," she said. "But once later in church we just happened to run into each other. I dropped something, he picked it up, and our eyes met. Something told us, something happened between us, that I had the thought I'd like to know him better. He had the same feeling. So then we met just to talk. I remember saying to myself, 'Now you're not going to get involved like that.' I can remember that so clearly. I talked to myself and said, 'Look, he's just a friend and I have this problem at home, but I'm not going to get involved like that.' It turned out he had a problem too."

"With his wife, you mean?"

"Yes. He told me that he was very unhappy with

her. It turned out that he had a bigger problem than I ever had. Of course, he's still with her even now, but I don't think they've had a relationship for years. They're just together for the kids' sake. I felt sorry for him. I know now that this often starts an affair. He needed someone to talk and feel close to, and so did I."

"Did you then see each other quite often?"

"Well, yes, but not a lot. We talked mostly by phone at first. (Of course we saw each other regularly at church every week.) Sometimes our phone conversations were pretty long, an hour or more."

"What were the things that drew you together?"

She was fully in her stride now, no longer hesitant, allowing me to drink my coffee and feeling relaxed, more certain of herself and facing the situation.

"I think a lot of it was the problems we ran into trying to keep our relationship secret, having to guard so many things we said. He would hear things from his wife which he would relay to me and vice versa. So we'd keep each other in the know. We shared everything. Problems at church, at home, our personal lives as well. And we became closer through all of this. But once it came out. His wife found out there was something going on."

"How long after you had been seeing each other did she discover it?"

"Oh, maybe a year. We were blamed for things that never happened."

"You mean your relationship had not become intimate and you were accused?"

"No, not that. It was conversations at the church about people. We denied having any talks at all, but this only brought us closer together because we'd have to check out stories. We were defending each other."

"So your relationship didn't stop after his wife found out something."

"She really didn't find out anything that much. But no, it didn't."

"And your husband?"

"Well, he was suspicious at times, but he never had anything to go on."

"How long did your relationship continue?"

"At least five years."

"And in all that time your husband didn't know?"

"No. He suspected a few things, but not that I was in love with someone else. Not until it was too late— and then he started divorce proceedings."

So here was a relationship that grew in intensity for several years until it precipitated a divorce. As I munched on a cookie, I asked her about the marriage during that time: "What happened to your marriage when this affair became more intense?"

"For one thing, I lost all feelings for my husband," she replied. "I became very cold to him, but I pretended to be responsive. Still, the more I pretended he would sense that something was wrong. He could see the changes in me. I couldn't really be affectionate to him, and I often moved away when he came close. Still for years I could not bring myself to talk about the real reason. I did different things to try and overcome the other relationship. I made resolves within myself, tried to become interested in my home, to improve my family life, but there was always something that drew me back to this married man."

"Didn't you see him regularly in church? That tends to make it rather difficult to put him out of your mind! So in spite of your efforts to stop, there he was all the time. . . ."

"Yes." She looked down. Then she continued: "The relationship became more intimate. We saw each other often during the years."

"What did this do to your faith? You went to church on Sunday while all this was happening. For years it was happening. Didn't that shake you up?"

"Well, I had a guilt complex, of course. With my strict background and the preaching I heard every week it wasn't easy. My married friend helped me with it, though. He made me see that God would understand somehow. 'I should not put myself down, because the Lord knows my heart,' he told me. Besides, we didn't become involved deliberately to hurt anyone. So he kept saying that I shouldn't feel so guilty. I do and I don't! It was strange. I know that this relationship shouldn't be, and yet—you may believe this or not—I still felt close to God. Through the whole thing. However, I know that the reason why I'm having so much trouble right now making a clean break of it is because of my faith. Something very strong is holding me and keeping me from making a commitment to this married man, even though I'm in the process of a divorce. Our marriage had become so tense that there was no point continuing. But now that I'm free, I just *can't* seem to go out and do what I thought I wanted to do."

It was because of the affair and her inability to relate in her marriage that her husband had given up. They sold their house and moved into different apartments. The older of the children was in college and the other with her.

"It would have been so much easier," she admitted, "if I could have told him when I first had those feelings. But a Christian isn't supposed to have such feelings, so we were taught! I didn't have the courage. He knew the man very well and they were friends. If I could have only opened up about it instead of living with this thing for so many years, it probably would have been different. We might not be separated now."

She mused for a moment, then continued:

"First my husband took it kind of hard. What happened was that he found some cards we had sent to each other. To the office, of course. I guess I'm sentimental. We did a lot of that over the years. I kept them in a private drawer and he found them in our home. So then I was forced to tell him that I cared about this married man. It almost seemed like a relief—for both of us. He needed something tangible to try and understand me. Now he realized why I had been so cold to him over the years."

"He was relieved?"

"Yes, and thankful in a way. Now he knew it wasn't just his imagination. Not that I ever said that it was his imagination, but I had disproved everything he ever thought he'd found out about our relationship. Of course I had to lie here and there to cover up, but I always managed somehow. I don't like that part either," she said remorsefully.

"Did you ever tell your husband the extent of your involvement?" I asked.

"No, not that. He probably wishes I would, but he

hasn't pressed me. He says it doesn't matter anymore to him. The thing that matters the most to him is that he knows the truth."

While she was in the process of her divorce, the married man remained with his family. I asked her about his intentions.

"He loves me and cares for me. He tells me that he is going to get a divorce. But we can't both do it at the same time. That wouldn't look very good at church. Our church particularly. People would never understand! And that is the one thing that bothers me very much. *Who would accept our relationship now or in the future?* I haven't resolved that in my own mind."

"And yet for those years while your affair blossomed"—I couldn't help but point this out to her—"he never started any divorce action."

"Five years ago he had younger children to consider. His children are older now."

The fact of the matter was that he had not taken any action during all those years, and she had made the first move. They were both still members of the church, a church with definite and fixed Biblical standards. I asked her again about her feelings in the pew on any given Sunday.

"It's underneath, and it gnaws at you. For me anyhow, maybe for him, too. I don't know. I know it's not the correct thing for two married people to be doing, but he didn't consider himself married in a way."

"But you did?"

"Yes," she said affirmatively. "I'd like to be able to say that I don't feel guilty, but every other week or so I hear about adultery, and I will say that every time

I hear that word I sort of—you know—cringe a little inside. And yet there is a lot more to it in your feelings. I'm not deliberately trying to hurt anyone, or myself. I wouldn't. But I'd feel disturbed and then I'd talk to the Lord about it. And if this relationship is not meant to be I ask him to take it away, but so far he hasn't. My feelings are still there."

She was really waiting it out at this indecisive time in her life, waiting for something to happen. As she poured some more coffee she said:

"I have to wait and see what my outcome is going to be. If he should separate I think there'll be more pressure on me."

"From him?"

"Yes."

"But with your upbringing, your church, your family, your faith in God, and your very strong religious ties, what will it mean when this pressure is exerted?"

"Trouble!" She laughed and seemed a little relieved. "I keep thinking, well, nobody can say anything after I'm divorced and he's free, and we wait six months and then start to date. But I'm afraid I'm fooling myself. It's not going to be as easy as all that. There have been a few things said already. Speculation, because of my divorce."

"So you'd almost have to begin all over again somewhere else," I said.

"For me it would be very difficult, if not impossible, to do it here," she admitted.

"Could you turn your back on this way of life, drop all your friends and relationships, and begin somewhere else—cold?"

She was quiet for a long while. I was moving

deeper into the dilemma she had struggled with for some years, and there was no resolution of it yet. Finally she spoke up again.

"I think I have mixed emotions on that one. Maybe I could, but in another way I couldn't. I have some very deep ties here, I've made good friends over the years. I don't know how I could leave them all. And there's my faith too. Sometimes I see this relationship as idolatry. I ask myself whether I love him more than I love God. And then I shove that question away."

In the meantime she had not been able to let her marriage dissolve completely either. In spite of her separation, she had seen her husband again, asked his forgiveness, and attempted to generate some feeling for him. He had mellowed and they were spending some time together, doing things together.

"I must say that I have changed in my feelings for my husband," she admitted. "Perhaps it's compassion or concern. I think we now have a friendship going, not a love affair. But we didn't have that much before. I couldn't stand to be around him, couldn't stand to have him touch me. It's not like that any longer. For over a year before we separated I moved away from him if he wanted to put his arms about me. Now we are kinder to each other. I search myself and I feel sorry for him, but I feel sorry for myself too. It worries me."

"But at least you're saying that there are improvements over a year ago. Where there was nothing then, there is something now."

She agreed and tried to resolve another part of the puzzle: "I keep thinking, why can't I just cut it off? Why can't I just forget it? Why do I struggle? Unless it's been through the encouragement I have received from counseling. I'm sure that's a lot of it. But what's the right thing to do?"

I couldn't help but point out again that she had moved much closer to her husband than she had been for some time—and that meant a rekindling of her affections. Maybe there would be a stronger fire in the future. I asked her why (for the first time in her life) she had sought professional help, and Christian counsel at that.

"I think it was because my husband had suggested it some time ago, and I thought it might be good for me. At least I could say to myself that I tried. It would help me to talk with someone who would be totally unbiased. In my own mind I couldn't think straight. I was all muddled. But the first time I came, I thought it would be my last. It didn't turn out that way."

"You thought you'd only have one session?"

"Well, you know, you don't know what you're getting into. I didn't know what it would be like. I didn't know what I was seeking, either."

"What did the counseling do for you, then?"

Again she stopped and searched her mind. "Well, it helped me to sort out my thinking. At least I know what my conflicts are!" She laughed pleasantly. "More coffee?" she asked.

I turned her down.

"I guess I've discovered some connections in my present life, which I never realized before, with my childhood. I came to see myself in a different light. I have begun to understand why I have done the things I have done, why I feel as I do, what my needs are, who I am. For one thing, I understand the causes much better."

"But in spite of this counseling your husband decided to start a divorce anyway?"

"He had already made that decision. He has pushed the whole thing."

"In your recent times together, have you seen any changes in him? Has he matured some?"

"Well, he went for counseling too, but very little. Not as much as I thought he should have. And he has changed some. He reads a little too, but actually he's happy with the way he is. I told him the other day that I thought we were both much better people than we were a year ago. We've changed and grown through this whole thing. We have more understanding of people and their problems, and I've been able to help some others during these months. At least you don't jump to conclusions. People are struggling with their problems and there are so many reasons for everything. . . ."

I returned to the issue before her.

"At this point are you still in a quandary as to which way your life will turn? You're not sure?"

"Mmm." It was a quiet but positive affirmation. "And this bothers me. You'd think I would be sure. I really wanted my freedom, but then I turned around and went back to something that had made me unhappy for many years. *Why?*"

"But at least it's not made you *that* unhappy now?"

"True, but it hasn't made me overjoyed either." She laughed again and shifted positions.

"At least it hasn't made you unhappy," I repeated. "In the meanwhile your feelings for the other man— are they still the same?"

"No." That was an interesting admission. She made it quickly, convincingly. "But they're still there," she added. "I wonder if my feelings are more out of concern for him. I don't want to hurt him either!"

That had been part of the problem throughout the years, not wanting to disappoint anyone. And yet a decision means disappointment for somebody. In a triangle someone always gets hurt.

"I love this married man, but I don't feel it down deep, as I once did. If I had completely broken off with my husband, which I couldn't do somehow, and the man I loved were completely free, which he isn't, perhaps I'd feel differently. Perhaps not. There'd be more pressure on me, as I said, but the way things are going right now, I've kind of tied myself up."

"Unconsciously perhaps?" I asked. "Maybe a part of you is saying that you can't let yourself go and marry this man, that somehow your vows and your faith and your life in God are at stake . . . ?"

I had to press the matter to allow her to see what the dilemma was really about. And she was well aware of what I was saying.

"By your actions," I added, "you are still working at your marriage. Perhaps your feelings aren't there yet, but what you're doing is very significant. You are seeing your husband regularly even though you're practically divorced."

Again she agreed. I asked her what therefore had precipitated the change in her feelings.

"Possibly people at church, many strong relationships, my faith. I know it is very strong, and no matter how I try to put it down, my faith pulls and tugs at me. My children too. They believe. I wonder what they will think if at the end of all this I marry someone else.

They know him, too, and his family. They know we were good friends but no more than that. But if he splits up his marriage, even though I don't feel responsible for that, people will read their own connotations into it."

"You do not feel responsible for breaking up his marriage?"

"I do not." She was very firm about that.

"And he doesn't feel responsible for breaking up yours?"

"No. But what people will think, how they will talk—that, plus my own children and what they will think of me, may hurt their faith in Christ, and that bothers me. You know, if the people at the church knew that I had been with a married man, they wouldn't have me in positions of leadership. They are friendly to me now, but I know they'd not be if they knew."

She waited again before she continued.

"In my own mind I've had to consider all that. I've even tried to resign from some of my jobs, but they won't hear of it. I don't have any good reasons, and I can't tell what the real reason is. But morally I feel I will eventually have to give them up."

"But if you give up this affair and seek God's pardon—why? There is no need if you believe God restores and renews us when we confess. At least at this point," I added, "it's kept you busy and involved."

"Yes."

"You do pray?"

"Yes, I do!"

"What kind of answers have you received?"

"That's a hard one," she said slowly. "The fact that I'm still where I am tells me something. I know it's the right thing to do for me, to keep working at the church. But sometimes I think I'm two people. I go one way and then the other. If I didn't have the responsibility, I wouldn't go to church. I'd probably find excuses not to attend."

"Here are these 'two people' fighting within you, as you say. Which one is going to win?"

She laughed.

"Well, some days it's the one and some days it's the other." That didn't answer the question, of course, and she was quite aware of it. I waited.

"Some days I think it would be so much better just to give it all up, do what I really want to do. And then, well, it's my actions (as you say) that keep me working on my marriage, attending church, believing. In fact, I tend to take on more jobs at church, to stay more involved. I suppose that tells you something."

I nodded agreement.

"And maybe this is what I really want. Then sometimes I question myself, 'What are you doing it for?' I like to keep active and with people. If I didn't do it, I'd be home, alone, miserable. I'd be feeling more sorry for myself."

By assuming these responsibilities at church, she was actually approaching the person she envisions emerging victorious from the conflict. The battle raged with her emotions, but something else of greater, perhaps eternal value, could not be denied. If only the emotions could be pulled along . . . Others who had taken similar excursions have found their way back.

I stood up to leave and thanked her for her frank conversation.

"Running away would solve it for the time being,"

she concluded as she showed me to the door, "but it would be a little hard to live with in the long run."

"Yes," I said, "in the *long* run . . ."

No. 3

"I want it to be very clear, especially in my case, that my emotional entanglement was not something which has been solved by sheer human effort. I am no superwoman, or super-Stoic or super-anything. If it were up to me I would be somewhere else right now! This is being solved *strictly*—and I don't mean to be pious or anything—by the grace of God and by my taking him at his word. If I had to live according to my own desires and needs, I would be doing something that would not be pleasing to God, something that would satisfy me. But he has brought me to the point where I realize that my chief aim here is not to please myself but to do his will."

She sat on the couch in my office with a Bible on her lap, talking about a living, loving God. She wanted so much to tell others, through her own experiences, that there is no human solution to emotional problems. She had obviously spent much time with her Bible, for she was able to quote it freely; and she said that through prayer she had overcome her struggles.

She was a charming person with a warm, happy smile. She enjoyed people, but she told me that as far as men were concerned she kept a safe distance. Yet her personal attractiveness drew men to her, and like the other women I interviewed she took care to always appear with her best foot forward, friendly, smartly dressed, and her hair nicely styled.

"I had to be completely down before I could stand up again. I had to take God so seriously, without seeing what would happen tomorrow, that he was able to work. I understand now that he is not as much concerned with what is happening right now as with the final product, with the goal. I mean, it would be great to be loved now, but if it can't be, it can't be. I would like to have that love in my marriage, but I don't have it. It would be lovely to have," she added wistfully.

"So you deny yourself any love in order to become the person God wants you to be?" I asked.

"Well, to *deny* sounds already like a terrible sacrifice," she said clearing her throat. "Yes, in a way it is a denial, because I am missing in an earthly way something that is my right from God. I believe that sex is a normal thing that God has given; but it is not a total denial since God fills us with other things. He proves himself sufficient even if earthly bliss and love aren't there."

I challenged her: "How can you say that God is sufficient for you and removes from you those normal human desires?"

"Well, first of all I must admit that they're not completely taken away. I am a very romantic person. I am very sensitive to people. But I also know that God has given me a protective armor. If I want to use it, fine. If I don't want to use it, I have a free will."

"If you let yourself go . . ."

"If I let myself go," she broke in, "and start fantasying, if I start living in the flesh as the Bible warns us, living in the sense that I don't consider the spiritual but only the carnal, then I'm very quickly down, because of the particular type of person I am. You know, what makes this all very exciting to me is that I am extremely sensitive to the romantic side of life, so that it would be very easy for me to get into this same problem again. I can start imagining something just by the way somebody is looking at me! But it is God and not me, or I would already have made more of many opportunities."

"Could this romantic involvement happen to you again?"

"Oh yes, definitely. But God is very real to me and I know him. And that has made the difference."

"The reason why you are sensitive to romance is because there isn't enough of it in your marriage?"

"Enough? Hardly any." She said it with a certain disappointment in her voice.

"If your marriage were satisfactory to you, would you not have these inclinations?"

"No, of course not. I wouldn't have the inclination to look at somebody else. I've always enjoyed people of both sexes, but I don't think I would ever have been interested. In fact, I would say that for twelve years of marriage I never considered anyone else, even though the marriage was pretty rocky from the start."

"Rocky in what way?"

"Well, rocky in the sense that emotionally we were not pulling together as a team. We were going in different directions even though we were living together."

"What made you start looking at a married man after all those years?"

"Now, I wasn't *intentionally* looking at any married man. I wasn't intentionally looking at anybody. We are told in the Bible that, when we are drawn away by our own lusts, then we fall into temptation. Then we sin. But looking for something, no, this was not even in my mind."

"You were unhappy in your marriage?"

"Yes, yes, and I still am." She laughed a little. She spoke quickly, a little more nervously, as we approached the heart of our talk.

"I went for some help. My basic desire was to love my husband through God's help and reach him for Christ."

"Do you mean that you went to a counselor?"

"Yes, a Christian counselor."

"To find out how you could bring your husband to Christ?"

"Yes, and how to be a good Christian wife. We had no financial problems, and he is a very good man, a good father. But we were never one, as the Bible teaches, spiritually. The spirit must be first and then the rest follows."

"But perhaps your marriage would have been more tolerable if you had experienced more physical closeness."

"More pleasurable, yes. But I'm willing to let that go for the sake of a spiritual union, even though there are times when the physical is extremely important. But I believe the spirit has control over the soul and the body, not the other way around."

I returned to the subject at hand: "So you went to a Christian counselor."

"Yes, he was a former minister who had gone into counseling, although he still taught the Bible. He traveled, teaching and speaking, and many Christians approached him for spiritual counsel. His reputation and depth moved me to seek him out. I could just as well have knelt down and prayed at home, which I did, but if I could share with a person who was very spiritual—that appealed to me."

"How long did you see him?"

"Several months."

"And then what happened?"

"Well, nothing really happened, but I felt very free with him. I knew that I was always looking forward to these times, because here was somebody who understood me. Occasionally he commented on how nice I looked. That pleased me and bothered me at the same time. I didn't think it was necessary, but being a woman it pleased me too. And that's very normal, isn't it?"

She laughed again as I nodded assent.

"Well, I realized at one point as I was praying that I shouldn't go in to see him anymore. I didn't know *why* yet, but I believe that it was the Holy Spirit warning me, and I could obey or not obey."

"You had this feeling . . ."

"I had this feeling"—again she broke in—"that I shouldn't go in for a while, so I canceled my next appointment. God was gracious. He was offering me a way out."

"As you look back now on this particular aspect of it, would you say that you broke your appointment because of what you yourself felt, or what you felt from him?"

"Both ways." She said it quickly. "There was a definite drawing power from both sides. It was nothing outward yet, only the first stages of temptation. I sensed a definite attraction going on back and forth. After a month he called me to see how things were, and when he asked whether I was coming in again I made another appointment. When I saw him he asked me why I didn't want to see him anymore, and that put me on the spot. I said that the Lord was probably trying to teach me certain things so that I could rely on the Lord more."

"Did you explain your feelings for him?"

"Oh, no. I didn't say anything about that. I have always been very careful, and he was very wise not to press me too much."

"And then you continued to see him?"

"Yes, but one day he mentioned that he was going to leave and set up a Christian counseling clinic in another city. That triggered something in me. I felt as if the bottom was dropping out. He was the only person who knew about me and I had relied on him so much. So I just stood there for a moment and he said that I could always correspond with him. He promised to write and if he came to town he would see me. Then he just put his arms around me and that was all and I left."

"Were you thinking about him a lot at home?"

"Yes, some. Because he was interested in me."

We discussed the next phase of the relationship at a slower pace. A correspondence began between them which grew steadily. There were cards and letters with special messages, the kind that a woman will respond to. A man skilled in counseling women certainly knows how to reach a woman's emotions and responses. She, in turn, kept the correspondence a secret.

"I didn't want my husband to know. So anyway,

he wrote long letters and I was glad to receive them. He shared his own interests about the Christian faith, what he was doing and so on, and they were my interests too."

She stopped to ponder her thoughts. Then she continued.

"There was always something very personal in his letters and I became confused—afraid and confused. I didn't know what to make of all this, and then he returned one time to visit the city."

Again she halted.

"I think the Lord was sending me all sorts of red lights," she continued, "but I was far too much interested in my own pursuit of happiness, so that I was ready to experiment with anything that would give me some satisfaction. I saw him. It wasn't right. I had all sorts of thoughts that were wrong. I looked at all the things I was missing in my life—and here I could have them! It was a very dangerous road. And at this point I must say that God withdrew himself."

"So when you met . . ."

"Well, we were just sitting there in my living room"—again she had anticipated my question—"and we talked for a while. I looked very helpless because I really felt it was not right. He looked at me a certain way, and it wasn't very long before we were embracing. Certain things happened in that embrace which had never happened with my husband, and he said things I had never heard from my husband. They were nice to hear, but I knew this was very wrong, even though it gave me pleasure. He came every day during this visit. It was definitely sin. If I think back I can still say it was very pleasurable, but it was still sin."

"You saw each other every day?"

"Yes, in my home. One time I met him at the hotel. I should not have done that, and I was really uncomfortable there, but it never went too far."

"It never became intimate?"

"Well, it became intimate up to a certain point, although we never had intercourse. For two people who are on fire it is difficult not to be interested in each other! You put a match on the straw and you know what happens."

"And after the week was over?"

"We continued our correspondence and I realized I was losing my faith. I was not much interested in God. That was strange for me, but it proves that sin separates us from God."

"You didn't want to pray?"

"No, I really didn't, I really didn't." She repeated it three more times. "I became a very miserable Christian."

"So now you looked forward to his correspondence."

"Very much so. He became the Number One person in my life. We also had long-distance phone calls."

"How long did this continue?"

"At least two years or so."

"Did you see each other again?"

"Occasionally, but we talked often on the phone."

"Do you pay the bills?"

"Yes."

"Then your husband didn't know about those calls."

"No, and those bills were very high. I put aside some household money to pay them. His letters came every day of the week."

"Every day?"

"Yes, almost every day. And they became very, very passionate! Even though I was busy doing things at the church, I was very miserable at the same time."

"How did this affect your marriage?"

"My husband didn't know."

"Did he think anything was wrong in your relationship?"

"Yes, but that had been wrong before. Our marriage was without intimacy. We were living apart most of the time."

"If this Christian counselor had remained here, where would your relationship have led?"

"Well, I don't know. It may have become far more serious. I know there was a drawing toward each other in many ways. I liked him very much and I think he liked me very much too."

"And yet you knew that he was married."

"Yes, I did."

"And that nothing could eventually result from it?"

"True, but when you are involved like this, that's the *last* thing you think about. You are so engrossed that you always hope that some circumstances will happen to make this relationship permanent."

"But it wasn't reality?"

"No, it wasn't reality," she admitted. "It was building on something without any foundation. Of course, I knew from what he said that there had been great conflict between him and his wife for many years, and I projected that perhaps they would not remain together. She went her own way and he kept himself so busy that he stayed away from home as much as possible. He was missing romance and love and so was I. I knew something wasn't right, or else he would not have been interested in me—unless he was a real crook, which I didn't believe."

Here she hesitated again, so we took a break in our conversation. I stopped the tape recorder and flipped the tape cassette over, and, after stretching, she continued.

"I believe that God intended to bring us both back to himself. He allowed us our foolishness for a while. I don't think He approved of it. My own self-interest became so strong that it had completely choked the life of the Spirit in me. The thoughts of this married man became my only happiness, my real purpose in life. We would read the Bible together, especially the Psalms. That is where this 'Christian' relationship is so misleading. I would never have been interested in the things of the world, but because he would explain the Bible to me this brought us closer together."

"And you were able to reconcile this relationship . . ."

"I was, I was. Up to a certain point. But I did become less and less interested in the things of God and in my own marriage. I was only interested in fulfilling this other person."

"You still managed your housework all right?"

"Yes, I managed. But on Saturdays everybody would be around, and I was always fearful when I saw the mailman. There was a sense of guilt that I was trying to repress. Besides, I was out watching for the mailman every day of the week. This gets you into a very frantic way of living, because you are always anticipating something that might happen and you're never really at peace. Not at all! Even in the midst of this lovely time, humanly speaking, I was fearful because I was married and here was something going on that just wasn't right. Whether I was happy or not was not the point. We were trying to carry on a relationship, yes, an adulterous relationship. We are told in the Bible that, if you *look* at a man or woman just with the thought of committing adultery, you have already committed it."

"Are you really saying that you were developing a sensuous look, or are you saying that you wanted a deep friendship?"

"I wanted more than a friendship at that time. Oh, yes! There is always a danger because we are in the flesh. We have this earthly house around us that draws us to things which are not right."

I questioned her about the change in the relationship, to discover what gave her the strength to turn her back on this married man and renew her life in God. This is how she framed her answer.

"We were very much engrossed. I was becoming centered on this person, thinking about him, reading and rereading all his letters until I knew them all by heart. I was very jumpy at home with my husband, even more so than before. God was trying to tell me that I was in the wrong, but I wasn't listening. So I believe that God in his great wisdom had to bring something about to shock me. He had to startle me and now I can praise him for it. It wasn't done in a kind, gentle way, because there was no such way to deal with this affair."

"You weren't about to end it on your own?"

"No, I wasn't. I was *enjoying* it. I probably would have gone very far with this person, if I had not received the strength God gave me to overcome. There would have been more physical involvement, I know that. The letters were just bubbling over and everything was said in those letters that could have been done somewhere else."

"Do you still have those letters?"

"Oh, heavens, no. I burned them all, each and every one of them. Things like that have to be destroyed. But what I mean to say is that this was not an innocent relationship just because it didn't end up in intercourse. Everything was said in detail in those letters, which is just as bad. It was delightful, but it was wrong. I should have had this kind of relationship with my husband."

She stopped again and tried to word carefully what came next.

"I had lunch with a Christian girl friend. She asked me some very personal questions. She was clever, and for the first time I confessed to her about this other person. She knew him also, and when I told her I was in love with him, she became white as a sheet and very quiet. I felt she was hiding something from me. She seemed very tense. Then I brought her to a point where she said that she could not reveal a certain secret, for she had promised never to talk about it. It turned out that she had had a relationship with him for many years, like husband and wife, and that she still had feelings for him. She said he was *the* love of her life."

I allowed her to keep on talking.

"I just couldn't believe what she was saying. I didn't know what to make of it. When I returned home I called him and said that I had found out something terrible.

When I told him he became terribly upset over the phone and said he would explain it on paper. His letter was full of apology. He said he was sorry that he had hurt me and that he needed God's forgiveness. He asked me to pray for him. At that point I wasn't interested in praying, but I really believe that the amazing grace of God began to reach me. I could very easily have taken the car and smashed myself up. I wanted to! I could have done it, too, because of my being taken up totally by this relationship. I had thought it would be something very permanent. And, when the whole thing was wiped out, I found God's arms there."

"Would you say that after you discovered these facts, you still retained your love feelings for him?"

"Oh, yes. You don't destroy those things in one day. I had angry moments, but I had some very nice thoughts too and they had to be healed. This was probably the dark night of my soul. I was truly unhappy in my marriage, I had just finished this other thing, but now God proved himself faithful and his love was much stronger than my failures. 'Love never fails'—that I know without the shadow of a doubt. If it hadn't been for his sustaining power, which I wasn't even asking for at this point—I was not even reaching out for God—I don't know what I might have done; but the Lord didn't let me do anything drastic. I was in a big mess, spiritually and emotionally."

"How did you step out of this?" I asked.

"Well, I didn't *just* step out of this. It wasn't that easy. And it's still hard today, a couple of years later. I must thank God for having allowed all this to happen, because even though I don't encourage anyone else to get involved, I can look back without shame since I know I have been forgiven. I have been reading in the Scriptures of other people who have been involved in things of this type, people after God's own heart. And yet he meant to work through these people. He used an awful lot of wicked people. Bad things which happen to us can be used for his glory, for our own good, and we can become instruments of God to help others. We can't just think of the wrong we've done because then we wind up in a rut. It took me a long time to realize that I could build again. I didn't want to think about the past because, the moment I would, I'd cry and feel sorry for myself. It's still easy to feel sorry for myself today, but God doesn't change and I look ahead."

"That kind of faith isn't easy to come by," I commented.

"No, no. This kind of faith can only be acquired through a very deep trial. The waters will not overflow you, as God has promised."

"Would you say that the biggest problem to overcome was your emotional entanglement?"

"Yes," she said candidly, "that was the hardest. As human beings we tend to want another person's care and warmth and love. We help each other, draw upon each other, and the healing process is very, very long. I do feel I am healed. That is, I am healed inasmuch as I am willing to *recognize* that I am, *believe* that I am healed. If I start thinking about the other person . . ."

"You still can?"

"Yes."

"In spite of what you now know about him?"

"Yes! I could stay here and create fantasies and

start building up on the wonder of what could have been. But I have to be very abrupt and believe God has healed me and stand upon what he has said. Then his Spirit enters and I look unto Christ, who is the author and finisher of my faith."

"Have you accomplished all this by your faith in Christ alone, or did you talk it over with another Christian?"

"Well, I did seek some counsel again later. I was looking for a woman counselor, hoping God would send me one. God built up my faith during this time, and I began to believe I was forgiven, but I didn't *feel* forgiven. Whenever this married man came to my mind, I would immediately ask God to take that thought away from me. And he would, but for me it was an exercise of the will. Occasionally I didn't let him and I went ahead with my fantasies, but then I would be miserable and cry."

"So you were looking for a woman counselor?"

"But I couldn't find one. Then I found a Christian minister whom I believed I could trust. That could have presented some problems too—I was very much afraid to talk with another man—but I needed help and I trusted God to lead me. Since I was still thinking of the other counselor, I needed to get rid of those thoughts."

"Therefore it was helpful for you to clarify this affair, air it with another person, so that you would not only believe in God's forgiveness but accept it in reality," I said.

"It has been good for me to be able to talk about this," she replied. "Still, my deepest help comes from my own relationship with Christ. You can go to a counselor for an hour, but he can't be with you all the rest of the time. Then what do you do? I was tempted to call this minister up between appointments, to talk with him about my problems, but I felt it was not right. So I leaned more and more on God and relied on him as my Wonderful Counselor."

I emphasized to her that I saw Christian counseling as a means of bringing about a personal reliance upon Christ, not the counselor. The counselor is an instrument through whom the love and acceptance of God reaches another person, but he dare not assume the role of God and take charge.

"Looking back now on your experience, how would you summarize it?" I asked.

"I must admit that it was the most wonderful thing that has happened to me in years. It was wrong, but it was still wonderful. When I think back on it I feel warm inside, if you know what I mean. 'The pleasures of sin are for a season.' This was a pleasurable thing, and I can't say even today that it wasn't! It was very warm, very kind, very affectionate, very meaningful, very loving. If we had ever lived together as husband and wife and faced problems, I don't know what we would have done, how we would have related. But this was like taking a trip to the Bahamas and having an affair on the boat. It's all very lovely, but it's not reality."

"But can you take the good out of it?"

"Well, the only good I can take out of it is this: I realize that God does not wipe me away because I have sinned. He does not turn his face from me, if I am willing to be led by him and repent of my wrongs. I can allow him to use me to build on this excursion something that is of lasting value. My desire now is to live for his glory, and for his glory alone, even though I have human desires and needs, which incidentally are not fulfilled. If I didn't have this daily relationship with God, I would be quite a different person. I would be very desperate. For me, life is not what I want it to be, and so I concentrate on the presence of Christ. 'He must increase, and I must decrease.' * This is really my biggest desire, and I know I'm on the right track."

I thanked her for the opportunity of allowing me to enter so deeply into her personal life. She closed her Bible and smiled. Again she emphasized that she had been willing to share this intimate story in order that someone else would find that same victory which she had won through Christ.

No. 4

"I was not looking for an affair. I don't even like the word. But mine was no ordinary affair, it was a first-class affair. We went to the best places, attended outstanding events, met sophisticated people. He had to be Mr. Perfect for me to fall. When you work in a man's world as I do, I could disqualify them all one by one for a word, a glance, their walk, a mannerism, anything. I wonder now if that has been a protective device for me. Anyway, he was Mr. Perfect, articulate, suave, handsome, kind, understanding—and I was looking so hard to find something wrong with him and *couldn't*."

I tried to picture her in her office, seated behind her desk, efficiently handling business matters. But we

* The quotation is from John 3:30, where John the Baptist speaks of Jesus.

were talking in her den and she had taken off her shoes, tucked her legs under her, and sunk down into the leather sofa. She was very much at ease as she confessed that to renew this story was like going to the dentist.

Her children were grown and had all left home. She certainly didn't show her age. That was probably due to her early start (she was married at the age of sixteen) and she looked alive, attractive, happy. She kept herself trim through her various sports activities, which accounted for her lithe appearance.

"I had a very careful training from my father, whom I really looked up to and still look up to. Because of his influence I did not believe in God, and the Bible was not correct. I was not brought up in the church, but after my children arrived my husband thought that they should have religious training. He was a nominal Christian, and I agreed that the children should have an opportunity to learn something—at least for the sake of comparison."

"Then you had no background in the church?"

"Not at all."

"You were married in a church?"

"No, in a wedding chapel."

"You decided after the children came to bring them up in the church?"

"Not *bring them up*. I thought it was good that they would have religious exposure. I was definitely a freethinker as far as philosophy was concerned, not as far as my morals go. I was always very ethical concerning my personal life, but I was really mixed up. I thought I had the answers—but I met these people in the church. One woman was praying for me, and she kept calling me, so I went to a Bible study and there I accepted Christ. Just before that decision my brother took an overdose. My mother called long distance and said there was no hope for him! I was driving home and I said to myself that, if my brother pulls through I'm going to have to do something—maybe there is a God. And he pulled through; the doctor said it was a miracle. My friend kept calling me and that's how I came to believe in Christ. Incidentally, my brother is a Christian now, too!"

"Were you married young?"

"Sixteen," she smiled. "That's pretty young."

"Do you think a person should marry that young?"

"No," she answered candidly, "but, as I said, I thought I had all the answers. And I could debate on a lot of different subjects and hold my own with adults. So I said to myself, 'Hey, I know what I'm doing.'"

"So you were pretty confident?"

"Yes."

"What happened to you when you became a Christian?"

"I found that my father was *wrong*." She smiled again. "And I really did change, even though I was in my late twenties. I expected my husband to follow along too, because there were problems in our marriage. We hadn't been able to communicate at all because he had a severe drinking problem."

"Already—in your early marriage?"

"Yes. It became more severe and more tense as time moved on. I felt that he would want to accept Christ too, and then the drinking would fall away. He joined the church with me but there was no change in him. So I knew that any changes would have to be within me, but I kept praying for him just the same."

"So he was attending church and drinking heavily?"

She nodded her head in agreement.

"Did that impair his work?" I asked.

"No, it did not, but it slowed him down. He was always tired."

"Did you discuss this drinking problem with him?"

"Oh, yes. Many, many times."

"What was his side of it?"

"According to him there was no problem. And we would end up in a shouting match and I would go off into my own space bubble. I just pretended he wasn't there. I withdrew from him, completely withdrew. Any physical relationship we had was mechanical—and very seldom. His thing was the wine and the television, and mine was the kids, church, house, working, Bible studies. I went out a lot. My life was very full. Music lessons when the kids were young, adult classes in the evenings for me when they were older, and then I'd just escape into my room with my books."

"Christian books?"

"Yes. I was very involved with the church. Very much 'on fire,' as they say. And they wanted me to be in this and that and president of the women's associations and so on."

"But in what way did the drinking become a problem if he worked steadily?" I kept on pressing.

"When someone has at least one bottle of wine every evening and falls asleep right after dinner . . ."

"Did drinking give him courage?"

"Perhaps. I would bring home books on alcoholism and put them all over the house, and he kept on saying, 'We don't have a problem.' But the next morning after an argument he would say, 'I'm not going to drink anymore. I'm all finished. All I want is cooperation. I want the house quiet, the kids quiet, and I expect cooperation *from you.*' You know, the alcoholic is always expecting it from the other person. And I'd answer, 'I'll do the best I can,' but he wanted superhuman performances from everyone."

She told me that he was a good provider and that she could count on him materially. He also encouraged church participation for the entire family, but she was already escaping the relationship by attending both Sunday morning and evening as well as teaching in the Sunday school.

"I kept thinking that we needed help," she continued. "My doctor told me that my husband was an alcoholic and would remain one all his life. I went to two different ministers. They wanted to come into the home and help but I was petrified. One drove by the house once and called from a phone booth and said, 'I know your husband is home. I saw his car and I'd like to come by and talk with him,' and I just stood there *shaking.* I was afraid of what my husband would do. Loud. Verbal. Caustic. He threatened me often and he'd try to manipulate me, so I didn't dare to bring anyone else in to talk to him. Why I allowed myself to remain intimidated by him as long as I did, I don't know."

"You were afraid of him?"

"Yes. I was really apprehensive. And so were the children. We did everything we could to keep life tranquil. We expected a miracle from God. We really prayed."

"How long did this continue?"

"About ten to twelve years after I became a Christian. Whenever I thought I couldn't go on any longer, he'd stop drinking for two or three days and we had some fellowship. Then there'd be a few good days."

After all the children entered school, she went into the business world and became very successful. She probably was a threat to her husband because of her capabilities. Perhaps that explains why he relied more heavily on stimulants.

"But I was scripted," she told me (having just read some books on transactional analysis). "I was scripted to remain married. My parents had always taught me to put down the self. I may not have had a religious upbringing, but I did have that from my family—and no divorce!"

"And your religious faith reinforced that."

"Yes, and three children! It was difficult to step out of the marriage with three children, and it seemed to me that I always kept things stable. I was the stabilizer in the family. But I started programming myself that, when my youngest turned sixteen, and if God had not performed the miracle in my husband, I would not continue any longer in the marriage. That long, but no longer. In my business I had my own car, I had my own money, and I spent all my spare time with the kids. He would try to make me feel inadequate, but I'd merely shut him out. Completely. And then I'd escape into my own world. I was successful in my business, I was successful at church, and I felt successful as a person."

As we approached the subject of her involvement with a married man, she began by telling me that she moved in a business world of men day after day. She was never tempted to take up with anyone in spite of the pressures of the home. Mr. Perfect didn't come along, since she always picked flaws in the life-styles of

66

all the men around her. In the meantime her husband traveled a great deal and decided to establish a new office in another city. When their youngest became sixteen they agreed to a separation, and she was facing facts—the facts of an impossible marriage.

"I thought, how fantastic, when we terminated our relationship. Why did I think he would go to pieces if I were to suggest a separation? Why had I waited this long? But there were days when he didn't even remember our conversation and started making plans again for our future. Then I began to realize how the alcohol kept him from living in reality."

She took a deep breath.

"There was quite a span of years," she continued, "when our relationship had been bad, but I always thought—to get involved, that's scary, that's committing adultery, and I don't want to do that! I wanted something very wholesome after the divorce was final. Yes, I wanted to get married again and to a Christian, but I had no plans on how to get there."

Her business took her to Saint Louis and she returned home on a late flight.

"I was really beat when I got on that plane and I decided to grab three seats and go to sleep. And, just before takeoff, there came this man aboard and sat next to me. I looked at him and turned away and thought, I'm not even going to talk to him. And that's how it began. The next thing I knew we had laughed and talked all the way across the country and were landing."

"You hadn't known each other before?"

"No, we just met on that plane. He had his own business. A brilliant man, conservative, a fine type of person, and we found we had a lot in common."

"A Christian?"

"Well, he attended church some, but he was not active. He knew there was a God but he didn't believe."

"You've always met men and been around men . . ."

"Yes, and I was never thinking about anything like this. You see, I didn't consider myself a sexual being. I was very turned off in our marriage. And yet I realized before we landed that we had been sitting there bumping arms the whole time. I was always very careful to keep my distance. I wasn't naïve about even little things, but I found myself responding to him."

"And then what happened?"

She laughed a little.

"Then—I got off the plane. It was morning. I looked back and saw him standing there with his little wife, but we had exchanged business cards and I was aware that during the whole trip we had touched kind of casually but nicely. He called me a few days later for lunch, and I thought that would be fun, and then I thought, 'Hey, wait a minute, what am I doing?' He asked, 'Shall I pick you up at the plant or would you rather rendezvous?' and I said, 'Rendezvous,' and it was very exciting. I could have stopped any time I wanted to—but I didn't want to! I was feeling things I never felt before, things I hadn't felt for a long time. The reason I chose to rendezvous was that I couldn't explain his presence in my business. People took me to lunch all the time, married men. It was part of the business world."

"But you knew there was something different about this?"

"Yes, I knew that."

"And after lunch?"

"We met for lunch again the same week."

"And then?"

"We had lunch again and the next thing I knew we were physically involved."

"How long did your relationship continue?"

"Over a year. It didn't end abruptly then. We are still friends, but it just faded away."

I probed a little further: "What were your thoughts during this affair?"

There was a long pause. Usually she was quick to answer; she spoke in a rapid pace that impressed me. She had everything well in hand and well thought out, but now she stopped to think.

"O.K. When I knew it was eventually going to happen, that I was going to commit adultery—and I never felt so attractive, and his marriage was very bad—my thoughts were, 'It's wrong.' I should pray that God would stop me and take away my desire, but I didn't. I didn't allow God to. I didn't want to. I would want to and then I *wouldn't* want to."

"You kept on teaching at church during this affair?"

"No, I didn't. Luckily it was the end of a quarter. I taught one more time and then gave it up. I couldn't do it! I felt very guilty. Yet I rationalized—we were very conservative and it wasn't frequent. At times we would meet for lunch and that was all and I could justify that."

"But it was still exciting to see him and be with him?"

"Right, but both of us didn't really want an affair.

We tried to be controlled, but it frightened me! I was a different person, you know, because of my responses. I thought before that I was totally dead, I really did, totally inadequate on a physical level, but now . . . And while I was with him everything was fine, but when our cars went in opposite directions I felt *terrible*. So I broke some luncheon dates, and then I'd think, 'Is he ever going to call me again?' And I'd die for two weeks! I kept reading books and articles on women who were having affairs, and I had never read things like that before. Never. The women always got hurt, and I thought, that's not going to happen to me because I'm going to end it before I get hurt. When we were together I looked ten years younger, I really sparkled. People noticed it, too."

"But didn't you mind being seen together?"

"I was seen with other men legitimately many times! But I wasn't laughing, I wasn't as happy."

"So you didn't worry about that?" I asked.

"No, because I have been seen in the business world for years when nothing was wrong. And we were discreet. But you know, some of the things I had been teaching about I saw happening in my own life."

"What do you mean by that?"

"I had recently taught a number of lessons on how Satan will attack us where we are vulnerable," she replied. "O.K., everyone is vulnerable, but I didn't expect myself to be vulnerable in *that* area. I thought I was strong. I thought that Christ meant so much to me that I could *never* engage in adultery. That's what really startled me, and then I started to rationalize. 'You've been turned off all these years,' I said to myself, 'and God understands that, too.' Then I'd say, 'But that's not right.' So I knew this all had to end."

"You were in conflict?"

"Oh, yes. I wasn't really happy, although I was happy whenever I was with him. So I thought I'd get my divorce and he'd get his, and then we'd have terrible guilt feelings. I realized that would never work out for me! I could see his little wife. They didn't communicate any better than we had."

"Is he still married?"

"Yes. He's at the same place now he was then."

"How did you break it off?"

"I just pulled away. We never had a discussion about it, but he'd call to get together for lunch and I'd accept, but when he called to confirm I'd break it. And then I knew it wasn't true love since in no way would I marry this man. I knew I was terribly infatuated with him."

She shifted around a bit and continued to talk.

"You see, he tried to get me to open up, to be honest with him, and I couldn't. I couldn't open up with him as I could later in a group or with my second husband. I couldn't discuss how I really felt inside. He wanted me to share my hostilities and tensions from my marriage, and I couldn't talk about that either. Then I realized that our relationship was very superficial."

"Because you couldn't relate to him as a person?"

"Yes. Physically we did relate. Intellectually we could relate. We had a lot of common ground to discuss. We had similar backgrounds, although he had no religion and I did. The thing that bothered me was that spiritually he wasn't where I was. Perhaps I was a stum-

bling block to him *by submitting!* We discussed that at
length and my work at the church, and he was very
concerned."

"Concerned that he would make you feel guilty?"
I asked.

"Yes," she said pensively.

"You assured him that the guilt wasn't because of
him?"

"Yes, I think I did," she answered thoughtfully.
"We got into that type of a discussion. I also knew that
he didn't share my faith in Christ. So spiritually we
weren't together. What we talked about was really of
the world: business, politics and so on. We were an
awful lot alike."

"In the meanwhile did your husband find out what
was going on?"

"No. He returned from a business trip and I said
I was going to see a lawyer and start a divorce. He said
that it was all right with him, and then later he didn't
want the divorce."

"Your relationship continued with the married man
during this period?"

"Yes, for several months. You know, we discussed
this. If we had met in college and dated we probably
would have married each other. Our outlooks were similar
and our interests were the same, but as far as I was concerned this was never going to work out."

"You knew that?"

"Yes, I knew that. And as I was drawing away from
him, seeing him less and less, my husband and I had a
final reconciliation, trying to make it work, but it didn't
last long."

72

"What about the married man? Were you thinking about him a lot?"

"I would just put him out of my mind," she said. "Then he'd call me again and I thought that was neat and would want to see him again. Once I took off for a business trip, and he schemed like mad to be with me in Denver. But he couldn't work his schedule out. And I was really glad! I was so glad he couldn't make it. I was all alone on my own and I decided, 'Now it's all over.' During these months I was also opening up to God, confessing my sins."

I realized that she was expressing how she felt as she tried to break off this relationship. When I asked her whether she really wanted it to be over, she replied:

"Yes, I really did. I wanted to have the strength to end it. I could say 'No' to him, but I wanted the *desire* to go away. It became less intense every time I saw him, because I really didn't want to have a close relationship with a married man. I was legally separated—but he wasn't, and I didn't feel right about it."

"But what if you had had that spiritual oneness with him?"

"It still wouldn't have been good. Maybe the good feelings would have lasted longer, but it would have been horrible! We would have had spiritual oneness and physical oneness, but he would still be married, and that would have been very bad."

She added another thought.

"Also, I didn't want to be the catalyst for his marriage to split. I didn't want that guilt heaped on me. I didn't want that at all. And when I was all alone on that business trip I had a really neat time. I saw a lot of temptation and I had no conflicts. I now realized that the inadequacies I had felt about myself were because of my marriage, but they were not in me. So I felt very confident as a woman, and I was chased by different men—but there was no temptation. Was God really helping me? I think so. Because I'll admit—I like being chased."

"So you were able to avoid any more entanglements because you wanted to be free."

"I wanted to be free," she repeated.

"And you discovered some strengths within yourself to meet temptation?"

"Yes."

"And when you returned from that trip?"

"He called me, but there was no more involvement. My husband turned around and divorced me because he said this would shake me up. I made up my mind that I would not become involved again. I was in control of my emotions. God had forgiven me and I went to church. I thought, 'Sin is sin.' It was a big sin, but God *has* forgiven me, and I'm not going to carry a burden of guilt around. I heard a sermon about letting go. I realized that I had to let go of my husband because that was an impossible situation, and I let go of this married man because that was going nowhere. And I felt that God was just taking it all away."

"When you saw him the last time, what did you say to him?"

"I discussed with him my position with Christ and how important that was to me. He said that he'd call me again soon. He didn't hear me. I didn't say that it was over but I said something like it. He didn't want to listen. He called occasionally after that, but I wouldn't always return his calls."

"Did you call him?"

"No. And we didn't meet anymore for lunch. Then I started going to a Christian group of single adults. Now, they weren't very exciting. I knew many more exciting people in the business world, but at least this was a step in the right direction."

"So when you closed the door on this relationship, you didn't have anyone else in your life?"

"No, there was no one else. I drew away gradually. I had to. I didn't want to wrench my heart. You know, I'd still be attracted to him, but not as much as I was."

"And he to you?"

"Yes. I just wasn't interested any longer. It tapered off so nicely over a year's time. I look back and ask, 'Who was I during those few months when it was so intense?' I wondered what was really happening."

"Do you understand that now?"

"Yes," she said quietly, "and I think it broke me. I can now read Psalm 51 and pray that prayer: 'Create in me a clean heart, O God; and renew a right spirit within me. . . . A broken and a contrite heart, O God, thou wilt not despise.' I wasn't broken before. I really wasn't. I always figured I could handle things somehow. I could pray and figure things out but now I'm more sensitive. All of a sudden I was tuned into the kids and their dating problems too. I was more sympathetic."

"How did you feel when you were in church and would hear a minister mention adultery?"

"It was like a knife—very uncomfortable. I always

felt guilty, but I knew enough of the Bible so that I could go home afterward and turn in my Bible and be comforted. I knew what I was doing was not right. Even to have lunch with a married man when you know he is superattracted to you is sin. And I was on an ego trip too. I knew that. But when I heard that sermon about letting go, I knew I had to let go of this married man, live alone, and face the responsibility. You have to do it alone, just with God."

She shared with me that, after she had disentangled herself from this affair, had let go completely, she did find someone else—a Christian man who had recently been divorced.

"I didn't feel any particular attraction to him at first, but I enjoyed talking with him. He was easy to approach, kind, tender, compassionate, a real Christian man. And he knows about this other thing. It was best to tell him because we became serious in time."

She has remarried. She believes she has gained new strength—and in the process she has discovered that she is very much of a woman.

"I am aware that there is a spiritual battle going on in the world," she concluded. "And we are caught up in that battle. If we want Christ to help us we have to let him, totally. And I think I would have had a lot of trouble getting close to my new husband had I not had this other relationship. It did bring me out of my dead, frightened self, a kind of resurrection. Out of sin there can be some benefit, some lesson."

Before leaving I commented that Augustine had written somewhere: "I dare to be bold to say that many a man has been the better for some sin." He didn't mean that we were to go out and commit as many sins as possible to become better persons, but that we can take out of a sinful relationship that which makes us more compassionate, more understanding, and more receptive to the grace of God.

"Every man feels more comfort and spiritual joy after true repentance for a sin, than he had in that innocence before he committed that sin." (John Donne)

2

Getting Over
an Emotional Involvement:
A Correspondence

A CERTAIN COUNSELING SITUATION developed during a
Christian conference and led to a follow-up correspondence. The conference itself had become a time for
one wife to unburden herself. She had carried a great
love for a married man which she already knew she had
to give up.

The affair occurred between two couples who were
very close friends with one another. They belonged to
the same church and often went out together socially.
The younger, more attractive wife fell in love with the
other husband, and the two of them became close intellectually, emotionally, physically, and even spiritually.
Their relationship grew in intensity, and they quite nat-
urally began to be disturbed in their larger friendship as
couples. Since all four were ardent Christians, these two
believed that the only honest thing to do would be to
bring this out into the open. So they shared the essence
of their relationship with both of their partners.

That was the beginning of the end of the affair, but
the emotional struggle of cutting loose and going back
into each family situation was only starting. Both couples had children. All shared a deep faith in Christ as
Lord and savior.

It is not my purpose in this life story to explore the

reasons why this affair blossomed, but to share the younger woman's letters of recovery. That correspondence lasted over a two-and-a-half-year period. It illustrates some of the heartaches and trials and delineates some of the steps she took toward wholeness. But, for background, let me add these factors.

The involved husband had a rather plain wife. She was kind, proper, and devout. He found the younger woman more attractive, alluring, and vivacious. She was, in fact, the very opposite of his own wife: interested in many things, bubbling over with an enthusiasm for life, and very exciting. But, in spite of her appealing personality, she balked at doing her share of the housework, she had an explosive temper, and she was very resentful of her own plodding and undemonstrative husband. She thought that he put up with her, tolerated her more than he seemed to appreciate her. She thought he did not really love her—at least, she did not feel loved and was stimulated in the presence of the other married man.

Her first letter arrived shortly after our counseling sessions. By this time the affair had been openly discussed among the four and a pulling back into reality had begun.

Dear Henk,

Thank you for your suggestion that I might write to you. Much has happened since our conversations. In retrospect I do not think I gave you a very fair picture of my husband. In a sense, all I told you was true but somehow not in quite the correct context. He is undemonstrative in his attitude to me, but his love is real. I knew that all along, but I was not willing to accept it. Since we talked he has attempted to put right some of the things which were worrying me. For example, we bought a place by the water about sixty miles from here for vacations. We have also talked about several other issues. I can but hope for more cooperation in the future. Your speaking to him made him do something about our problems.

Perhaps the greatest development, however, is with the other couple. The husband has accepted a new position, and he is looking forward with tremendous enthusiasm to that. It is quite a promotion for him. He will be happy and find much fulfillment in his work. The only thing that disturbs him is that he will move away from me, but then that may be our solution!

I spent some time with his wife last week, sorting out some of the things which had upset us both. This was extremely difficult for us, as we were grappling with aspects which touched us at the very root of our being. But for both of us it was worthwhile. Because she did not really understand what had happened, she could not forgive me, nor could she forgive him. She could not trust him or accept him. For all of this she hated herself. But now there can be a work of reconciliation between us all. We have been so conscious of God's Spirit at work in our lives.

I have thought much about your illustration, you know, the bit about the two brothers. The one who had been the prodigal had really experienced the love, forgiveness, and mercy of God. I now know how grateful and renewed he must have felt. For the other it was merely a fact in which he believed.

Thank you for so very much. God is at work in our situation.

Best wishes! ...

The second letter arrived a few months later. One of her children had become very sick and that demanded a great deal from her. As the illness lingered for some weeks, it became increasingly difficult for her and she reflected on it.

Dear Henk,

I want to let you know how matters stand in regard to the big confession session I had with you. Thank you for your letter in reply to mine.

The other couple has moved. They are about one hundred miles away from us. Basically, this is the only way this whole thing could go. We both realized, too, that while he remained here the temptation to contact each other would remain too great. Now the break has been made and only good can come from this.

The thought has come to me—why has my son's illness followed so closely in the wake of this very traumatic experience? I can only believe that it is God's way of helping me to accept his way for my life completely! I had decided to fill the void which followed his departure with a whole programming of activities—to sort of help me forget, to squash it out of my thinking. But God seems to be saying that I have got to deal with the problem *at its root,* to live with myself and not run away from myself. You know, to stop doing things for God but simply to *be* for him.

For someone like myself to have to cut my speed of living down to going at his pace, to know that he has to be surrounded at all times by peace and calmness—these are about the most difficult things that God could ask of me. I find myself having to do everything for him. He can't even feed himself when he is so weak. Any upset or churning on my part upsets him. This means a deterioration in his condition. So I have got to be at peace with myself. This is hard.

Before I mentioned to you that I was sure your sensitivity to people was born and nurtured through deep experiences. Perhaps this is what is happening to me now. The one experience with my lover where I only thought of myself and my own desires was followed hard by one where the needs of a child have priority over any wishes of my own. Isn't this living through a sort of Calvary, where the needs of others take precedence over one's own? And if Christ battled with this problem of self-will, how much more do we battle with ours?

Please do not think I am good. I'm not. I am battling, but I know that this is God's will for my life and I am trying to accept it in depth. You might as well know that I often long very much for him, even though we are separated by so many miles. The void is still there. God does not make it easy for us. We have to do his will even when it is difficult and very nearly breaking us. Neither of us will go back on what we have decided to be right for our lives—to return to our families and break off our relationship. And this simply because we have both given our lives to Christ.

Throughout all this my husband has been a tower of strength. He has subconsciously known that I have had very deep struggles with myself, but he has never doubted me, has forgiven me and just helped me to go on. Although my thoughts often wander, his steady acceptance of me is beginning to leave its mark.

These past months have been the most difficult in my whole life! But perhaps I might be fit for God at some stage. This letter has been all about myself. I think you will understand. Just telling you helps me to formulate the jagged thoughts milling about at the back of my mind.

Yours...

One of the letters which I wrote in return was an attempt not only to analyze and penetrate the issue, but it was also meant to give her further guidance. That is why I want to share a portion of it in this correspondence.

Dear...,

Perhaps you will be interested to know that presently I am counseling with three people who are desperately trying to overcome situations similar to your own!

Has it ever occurred to you that your affair was an attempt to escape from reality? From life, family, homemaking, the church, even God? The fascinating intellectual and emotional stimulation of your relationship probably obscured any such thought. It seemed so real. And yet look at the other side of it. You do not find much fulfillment in running a household, since you don't like those routine responsibilities which are thrust upon you. Therefore, was this romantic entanglement an escape from all these unpleasant duties? A nonacceptance of life made you vulnerable to something different, exciting, and escapist.

But there is something else. This rebellion against convention was an indication of hostilities which already existed within you. The affair was a symptom of your inner dissatisfactions. So you must have raised such questions as: Why am I dissatisfied? Why do I seek to escape? Why did I get into this affair? Why do I shun the responsibilities of being a wife and mother? Why, also, am I willing to throw everything out the window for my desires?

The answer to these questions does not really lie outside of yourself, not in your husband or his lack of affection, nor in the difficulties of being a wife and mother. The answer lies within you. You have certain basic emotional needs which can never be met completely by another person, but only by God *and* an understanding husband *and* a proper facing of yourself. To understand both your hostilities (which led you into this affair) and your needs is absolutely essential for complete emotional health.

Of course, it's a battle for you, but allow me to correct one of your statements. You said that you were not good. I say that in trying to accept God's will for your life you are choosing the good. Nothing can be gained by breaking up your home or the other. You could never live with yourself if you had done that. So this is right and you know it is right, and therefore the good within you (God) is triumphant.

Will it help you in this battle to think of the longing for your lover as an escape, as a desire to be free from responsibility, family, church, God—everything that you believe in? Of course, you cannot actually escape, for even if you went with the man you love there would be a house to clean and a family to take care of. On top of that an additional burden of guilt and you don't know how many other problems!

I want you to know that I'm encouraged by the progress you're making. You are doing well, even though it's taking a long time. And I know that you are gaining because of this experience. In years to come you will look back and be grateful for its contribution to your life, for I believe that, *though sin is shown to be wide and deep, thank God His grace is wider and deeper still!* (Rom. 5:20, Phillips)

Sincerely,
Henk

Her reply was long in coming, for she had sincerely wrestled with the contents of my letter. When she did write, this is what she said:

Dear Henk,
This letter is mainly a reply to yours of several months ago. It was a long letter in which you said much, most of which spoke straight to me. I have read and reread it many times. Once again I would

like to share my thinking and experiences with you.

Probably you realize how deeply my friend and I were involved with each other, more than we did ourselves! And this involvement had its sources in frustrations which existed before, within ourselves and our marriages.

When we both realized that to continue living in the same city was more than either of us could stand, his move was the obvious answer. Otherwise, all that we had built up over the years would be smashed. The move nearly broke us both, but we have lived through it, all the time not showing too much on the outside but experiencing deep trauma within. We knew that this was the path we *had* to go and merely prayed for strength to accept it.

This happened nine months ago. We have seen each other a few times during these months, sometimes alone, sometimes with both our partners present. These times have helped us to work this whole thing out of our systems, and then to get into them a more correct perspective, in relationship to our respective partners. Each time we have seen each other we have both realized that we have entered a new relationship, one more in keeping with reality.

You were correct when you said that for us both this affair was an escape from reality. We both knew this all the time. While we safeguarded our home positions with care, we continued the friendship under safe cover.

You also said that the way back is a long way. Very long! In some ways there is no direct road. The relationship I have now with my husband is a new one. I doubt whether much has changed for him, but lots and lots has changed for me! Many of the old tensions which existed in the past, as well as those with which I was battling when you and I talked, have now resolved themselves. Probably he has changed too, which has contributed toward a greater acceptance of him for me. Whatever reasons there are, much has been accomplished in a positive way. Indeed we have much for which to thank God.

When you saw me I was probably at my lowest ebb spiritually and emotionally. I felt I was being pulled in so many directions that I had lost myself completely. Now a year later I wonder if you would recognize me for the same person. There has been a deep healing of my spirit with my husband, my family, my attitude to life, which includes the church and God. That rebellion of which you were conscious is largely something of the past.

I will confess that at this time I still correspond regularly with him. There are many frustrations with which we both have to come to grips. From a purely practical point of view he was in a position more than anyone else to help me and I to help him. We were able to understand each other, even counsel each other. Because he has a very deep respect for my husband, he could help me to understand some of the frustrations and tensions under which my husband works in his job and how they react upon him, the man, the husband, the father.

Perhaps I have been able to help him understand what it means to a wife, to be left alone day after day and evenings, and so help him in his own home situation. Because, through correspondence, we have been able to say many of the things which lie very deep within ourselves, things we have found it difficult to express and understand, we have both been conscious of a healing process.

It is quite possible that within a short while we will, by mutual consent, cease to correspond. As you can imagine it has a certain element of risk.

I wish I could tell you about the change in my husband. Here, too, you will find it difficult to recognize him as the same person. He is more responsible, kind but firm, and has a deep reliance on Scripture. Our son is back at school and completely well, for which we thank God.

With love from all of us . . .

Her final letter contained the closing chapter of a two-and-a-half-year correspondence.

Dear Henk,

Your counseling by correspondence has helped tremendously, and I much appreciate it. My poor, starved spirit just absorbed it all. This is, I hope, the concluding chapter of the whole affair. My married friend and I have now stopped writing to each other by common consent, mostly because we knew that while we continued to communicate we were limiting the degree of effectiveness in our lives.

I do not think that he has sorted out his life to what it should be. He still needs quite a lot of understanding and guidance, which, unfortunately, I do not think he will get from his marriage. But it is *not my place* to give it to him! God is with him, as God is with me. Our continuing friendship throws our lives into jeopardy and threatens to completely paralyze our faith and commitment to Christ. I do feel very weary as a result of the tremendous emotional strain of the past years, but we do serve a fantastic God. His ways are perfect.

As far as my husband and I are concerned, things are increasingly improving. This period has helped us to get rid of an awful amount of frustration, bitterness, misunderstanding, prejudice, and mistrust. And slowly, just as you said, a new relationship is growing out of the old. Some of the old irritations and frustrations are still there, but they don't seem so big and important at the moment. I still sometimes get very angry with him, but it's not the same utterly desperate temper. It has more feeling and understanding. Maybe it will still come completely right.

These have been very rich, full years for me, and the person who writes now is different from the neurotic, unbalanced girl you saw over two years ago. Much of the rebellion has gone (although there is a little bit left, and who knows when it might appear again?), and a greater peace and maturity have taken its place.

It is with deep gratitude that I write this letter. May some of what I have learned through this experience find expression in my dealings with others. Your sensitivity comes from bitter experience— that's why it's real.

May God use you in his ministry in ever-widening circles.

With love . . .

3
Needs and Desires

As I REVIEW these intimate conversations in my mind, several common characteristics emerge. I found every one of these women very attractive. Not one was over-weight, sloppy, negligent, or careless of her appearance. To the contrary: each one showed off her figure in well-chosen modes of dress; usually her hair was tastefully styled; and she did the most with whatever gifts she was blessed with!

Each one revealed herself to be a warm person who was capable of giving as well as receiving love. But there were frustrations and hurts because deep inner needs were not met. This made these women vulnerable. The roots of these needs go down into painful child-hood experiences, the memory of neglect, the lack of acceptance, the pain of rejections. Any person who was given very little kindness and understanding, who sel-dom hears encouragement or receives love, will respond when a little kindness and love are shown her. Then feel-ings which have long lain buried are quickly aroused like dry wood responding to the flame—and many a man knows from experience how to reach such a woman by the kind of things he says or writes or does to ignite her feelings.

A Christian is therefore quite surprised when these emotions suddenly inflame, when barriers which have long been in place—barriers forbidding adultery or any other fleshly sins—fall before a bit of understanding and acceptance. We are shocked and surprised, and yet along with that shock may come a great sense of release. All those dormant emotions have now been liberated, and for the first time the frustrated, needy wife experiences pleasure, yes, and more than pleasure—love. That freeing of the emotions may explain why a love affair often lasts so long and is so difficult to break off!

The length and the struggle: "I should pray that God would stop me and take away my desires, but I didn't," confesses one of the women in these pages. "I didn't allow God to. I didn't want to. I wanted to and then I wouldn't want to." This was an almost frightening revelation, since a woman in love is caught in conflicting desires. Some very basic needs are being met by that married man, and yet she knows it is not right. She dimly desires to change her life back but encounters even stronger desires to experience more love and acceptance! Besides the marriage itself seems to hold out so little promise of any love and communication. This is the struggle of the woman in love with a married man.

"I had a picture of him that I looked at daily," she said. "First I tried to go one day without looking at it, then two days, then several days. There were some days I *had to* look at it, but now I never look at it anymore." That was a long time coming. Only as she began to face herself was she able to free herself and move in the direction which she knew to be right. But it is undoubtedly true that, when the conflict is resolved, a woman who has been in love with a married man is a better person because of that experience. That may be challenged by some, but I found it invariably so in these women, just as the truly repentant person is far more humble than the average Christian.

Another common characteristic of these affairs makes me want to underline the depths of the involvement. They are *total* in their absorption. Some are very sensual, sexual, intimately fulfilling relationships. Some are partially so, with only limited times of intimacy or perhaps no intercourse at all. Some remain like castles in the air, entirely in the mind. There are relationships which last for years; others last a matter of months. (A sudden meeting that turns into a one-night stand can hardly be called a love affair. I'm not including those frustrating encounters.) No matter how long or how close, these all become *affairs of the heart*. The emotional depths that are touched are just as great for the person whose affair seems quite proper and contained as for the one who is unreservedly sexual.

A few women I have counseled imagine the love relationship mostly in their minds. It is very real to them, but it must be labeled as fantasy. There is surprisingly little happening with this married man—a chance meeting at church or at work, a few words, perhaps a touch, a hug, a flirtatious look. A woman in love starts building on these slim encounters until they turn into reality. I am not talking about people in mental institutions but in the community. They relive chance meetings and build them up into romantic encounters. They become daydreamers, spending extra hours in bed, neglecting home and family, listening to romantic music, and looking at the soap operas on television.

"I wished I could get out of my cage," said one woman, "but my fantasy began to take on forms of reality. I actually thought that someday I would marry him! And all along I actually believed that I *deserved* my fantasies. Like a consolation prize. Life was so difficult at home and this was my only escape, my only happiness. Because of that happiness I held onto my dreams, but now I know that I can't have both fantasy and reality. Fantasy is mind without action! And reality, with all of its pain, is of more value."

So the affair, no matter how intense, really exists in the heart. And for this woman to overcome her fantasy was as difficult as it was for any of the women whose stories are told in these chapters. In most of these emotional traumas, if she is to find any solution, a woman in love needs some outside counsel. When she does not seek it, she is likely to follow her awakened desires into an action she may later regret. Not necessarily, of course, but suddenly aroused emotions are no guarantee for lasting happiness either! It is wise to talk it over with someone who can be cool and objective.

An affair may in reality be no more than a bargain. One counselor explained to me that women are usually more interested in warmth, security, and love than they are in sex, but they will trade sex in order to get that feeling of belonging. On the other hand, men are more interested in sex than they are in love, so they will trade love with words or little deeds in order to experience sexual excitement. So an affair turns into a bargain, a kind of trade agreement on the unconscious level. Viewed in that light, the relationship sounds hardly as fantastic as it may appear on the surface. It can't even be called "love." Some may argue that the bargain is well worth it. It's enough for them. But anyone who settles for a bargain when he could experience love and reality is satisfied with pork and beans when he could have a full-course steak dinner.

A good counselor, therefore, allows you the freedom to air your problem, to sort yourself out, to express your emotions, to become aware of what is really happening inside of you. The women I talked with had willingly entered that process, and, although the outcome was hardly similar for all, they were better persons for having faced their inner selves. To become aware of the thorns that grow up in the field of our hearts, to pull up any weeds of bitterness and hurt, to feed the ever-growing human needs with purpose and love, this becomes necessary action in times of crisis.

A woman in conflict who seeks counsel from a Christian already confesses thereby that she wants God's will for her life. She wants additional input and direction to overcome her inner turmoil. She often battles what she has been taught from the Bible, since it contradicts what she is feeling and wants to do—perhaps to divorce and remarry. There may indeed be situations where to perpetuate a marriage in which mounting hostility, resentment, anger, and malice destroy the members of the family—that may be worse than a divorce. This is not to say that I for one counsel that people should obtain a divorce. I do not. The problem is usually that we're not faced with two *good* choices, but with two mediocre, perhaps even bad, choices.

What would you say to a wife whose husband of

some years attempted to strangle her because she had had enough of his affairs and asked him to give up his latest paramour? And he refused and grabbed her by the throat! Afraid for her life, she divorced him and some years later remarried. But the more such a person believes in the Bible, the more she has been taught that divorce is against the will of God and that a Christian is never allowed to remarry, the greater is the need for Christian counseling. We need to come to grips with the law of God in and through the person of Jesus, whose love and compassionate understanding of human frailty is the focal point for all of Scripture.

It is absolutely essential to weigh what happens in any marriage, to evaluate the damage that two people do to one another, to appraise the brokenness of relationships. I am quite aware of the fact that some Christians may consider these words as an excuse to pull out of their family ties and jump into another relationship which seems so right and feels so good. Besides, what else is holding the marriage together except that they can't afford to divorce and "what people will say"?

On the other hand, we need to be reminded how the different types of love relate to both marriage and an affair. The Greeks spoke about *eros*, which is erotic, sensual, romantic love; *philia*, which is friendship; and *agape*, the love a marriage should be built on—for better, for worse, for richer, for poorer, and so on. God loves us with a redeeming, healing love which we do not deserve (agape). A marriage which has lost all three types of love may be replaced by an affair which has erotic, romantic love and perhaps good communication and friendship. But does it contain any self-giving, undeserving agape love? Is not that lover quite friendly and warm and therefore very easy to love? Only the love for someone who is undeserving can heal a marriage. When we are willing to put into practice the love God shows us, forgiving our husband or wife, then with time friendship and communication can be reestablished and erotic feelings may be resurrected.

C. S. Lewis points out that love isn't everything in marriage. Marriage also involves making a promise to one another, a commitment.

> The idea that "being in love" is the only reason for remaining married really leaves no room for marriage as a contract or promise at all. . . . If love is the whole thing, then the promise can add nothing; and if it adds nothing, then it should not be made. . . . And, of course, the promise, made when I am in love and because I am in love, to be true to the beloved as long as I live, commits one to being true even if I cease to be in love. A promise must be about things that I can do, about actions: no one can promise to go on feeling in a certain way. He might as well promise never to have a headache or always to feel hungry.*

The women whose stories appear in these pages were all Christians who held a personal faith in Christ and wrestled with their emotional attachments. To know that they *shouldn't* feel this way was one thing. That they actually *did* feel this way was another. How to

* C. S. Lewis, *Mere Christianity* (New York: The Macmillan Company, 1958), p. 83.

overcome those strong emotions became the battle in their souls. It led to intense suffering, an inner turmoil with the question—"How do I give up what I don't want to give up?" They desired a change—and yet lacked the motivation to make that change.

To change an emotion is the most difficult of all problems. No one can change the emotions of another. We are powerless to help, for each one must make the change himself or herself. One wife penned these lines to the other married man in her life:

I'm thinking a great deal about us tonight. Memories are beautiful but also painful. I never knew what true love was until you. You have always made me feel so wanted and needed. Thank you for that.

The only reason I can think of for giving you up at this time and trying to make my marriage work is that I don't feel I can bear the burden of the heartache so many people will go through in the breakup of our marriages and our being together. It's going to take a long time for us to get used to not having one another, if we ever do. The tenderness we have shown each other, the kindness, the thoughtfulness, the special days, the dreams we had will always be in my heart, and I will always thank God for you. As I think on these things now my heart aches. You know you have been my life and I have been yours.

I can only say that, if we can somehow turn these wonderful feelings toward our own partners and work our way back, maybe it will make our dreams' not coming true more bearable because we will be making someone else happy and no one else unhappy. You, my darling, have helped me overcome so many things in my own life. The true love you have shown me will not be forgotten. There is so much more I could pen at this time but . . .

The letter breaks off. She never sent it to him. That only illustrates the depth of her conflict and the paralyzing effect it had on making a choice.

Looking back on these intense emotional encounters, it is fair to say that each woman gained insight and meaning from her involvement. She did not just learn a lesson but she became a better person! *I dare be bold to say that many a man has been the better for some sin* . . . (Augustine). I found each woman a transformed Christian who had a new understanding of human frailty, a greater sensitivity to the trials and temptations of others, as well as a humbling experience of the mercy and goodness of God. The awareness of God, the love of Christ, and the desire to live the Christian life had reached new heights.

4

Counseling the Woman in Love: An Interview with Dr. John C. Mebane

DR. JOHN C. MEBANE is a friend of some years' standing. When he was in private practice as a psychiatrist in Hollywood, California, we often collaborated on certain counseling situations and shared our own problems with one another as well. When he moved to Hilo to become the head of the Mental Health Service for the island of Hawaii under the State Department, I felt a keen sense of loss.

Recently when I was in Hawaii to speak and teach, I flew over to Hilo. John picked me up at the airport and drove me to his old, spacious home which had been built by an Italian for his Hawaiian bride. We sat in a wood-paneled living room with a high ceiling, looking out at the lush, green vegetation in his garden. He had removed his shoes and was very relaxed as we sipped coffee and talked, while the tape recorder silently eavesdropped.

"How would you counsel a woman who is emotionally involved with a married man?" I began.

"To a certain extent it matters for what reason she has come to see me. For example, if she is referred by a minister this already tells me that she has some contact with the church, and it may become a springboard for what I would want to accomplish with her. If she comes on her own initiative or because of a doctor or friend, this indicates a certain degree of isolation. At any rate, the first step would be to get a history, do a lot of listening, and discover how her present situation relates to her past. This isn't always easy, because she is in turmoil and can't be very objective."

"Do you think that the person who usually comes to you because of an emotional conflict is interested in giving you all this data, or would she rather just get on to the problem at hand?"

"That depends," he said. "A person can be really shocked by this situation in her life. She's hurting, guilty, and humiliated and wants to know how it happened. That's a very good counseling situation. At other times, a woman comes in wanting to manipulate the psychiatrist. She wants him to say, 'You poor thing, you've had an unhappy marriage, you've been badly treated and this other fellow really loves you, so you're doing the right thing.' I've had married women in love with someone else come in and literally deposit their husbands on my doorstep, saying: "Do something about him.' "

"After gathering this data, what happens next?"

"You come to a stage of going over things with her, trying to get her to reflect. A woman who is deeply involved with a married man and comes to you for help is reaching out. You can assume a certain seeking on her part, a loneliness. If this woman is alienated in her own marriage and has found a meaningful bond with a married man, you may be able to dilute that bond somewhat by her growing relationship with yourself as a counselor. This may promote greater objectivity. An important part of counseling is to get her to feel comfortable and secure with you, so that she doesn't look to her newly found love as *the* source of support in her life."

"To relate to another person in a meaningful way—this is what you're saying?"

"Yes. This is fraught with problems too, because you have a woman who is unhappy, who is reaching out, and she may reach out for you. Somehow you have to keep yourself conscious of the maneuvering that may go on along those lines. You must remain a warm, positive person to her and keep her pointed in the direction of seeing her situation just as objectively as she can. I hear myself quite often saying to such a person that she may want to look back on this situation five years from now with the feeling that she did everything possible to understand herself. In other words, get her to hold still and look at the long-range picture, instead of impulsively acting because she is discouraged or disgusted now."

"Is there another stage after data gathering, reflecting, and maintaining a good, counseling relationship?"

"Yes," replied Dr. Mebane, "you then get to the stage of trying to work this through in some satisfactory manner. And this may take a long time, depending on the particular circumstances."

"Let's look at some of the causes. Why does a woman become involved like this? You have pointed to a bad marriage, loneliness, a reaching out . . ."

"All kinds of reasons! It could be a marriage which should not have been in the first place, or one that started out reasonably well but which has been badly strained by great incompatibility, the problems of raising children, the responsibilities of a family. I think a woman's expectations as she goes through her late adolescence and early adulthood are tremendously important. If she is encouraged to enter some kind of a career, then marriage can become a real trap for her, especially if there are children. Another reason is our *continuing expectations* in life. We are always looking for something more. Many people are dissatisfied with the present and they are seeking happiness."

"Why?" I asked.

"You can blame television, the media, Madison Avenue—because they say that if things aren't good you can work out some quick solution for them. And, therefore, when you are dissatisfied there's a great temptation to start shaking things up, reaching out to relieve your tensions."

"How can anyone change those unrealistic expectations?"

"If I can get someone seriously involved in counseling like this, I always try to get her to look deep within her own psyche for some greater integration of her total being. The volcano of an extramarital relationship may indicate a lot of action on the outside, but the eruption is really going on inside. And what I try to do in my counseling is to get her to see this as an effort toward spiritual wholeness. The changes she would like to make in her life situation for which she looks to her lover are really changes that must take place within her."

"Are you saying, then, that a married woman reaching out like this could be actually seeking wholeness, spiritual reality?"

"Yes, exactly," Dr. Mebane answered emphatically. "If this relationship ruptures the existing marriage and leads to another marriage, there will be the same disappointments, inner problems, and possibly some new ones. I don't think you solve that many things. And if there is a succession of these marriages, then you come face to face with what you're really struggling with as your own problems. Another man is not going to rescue this troubled woman and lift her to a new level of existence."

"Of course, she thinks at the time he *will* rescue her."

"Oh, absolutely! You know, there's one thing about counseling—if the woman will continue week after week, month after month, she will begin to realize that he is just a man! And she may see that he could have more problems than the man she's married to. And then the whole thing begins to fit into perspective. Now, I'm not saying that you couldn't find an unusual situation where a woman has a *terrible* marriage and she meets someone where there is an honest degree of compatibility. But most of the time, though, she is chasing a rainbow."

"But, while she's chasing a rainbow, it is a deeply emotional involvement with her lover—so, then, how do you change an emotion?"

"Of course, this emotional state doesn't last indefinitely. Someone who is seriously trying to understand herself better will in time become more objective. A woman who is more mature and does not have the illusions of a twenty-year-old can look at this third party as a person who has problems. She also knows that this relationship is without all the encumbrances of family illnesses, dishes, kids, and so on—idealistic—and that's not life."

"Are you saying, then, that you don't attack an

emotion head on, but you attempt to change the emotion by discovering its causes?"

"Well, this is the fascinating thing—if you look at this relationship as a struggle toward spiritual wholeness, then this feeling of love is a feeling we all ought to have more often! But I don't think we should have it in this kind of a situation. What we all seek is a personal relationship with God! If someone can feel this way even through this kind of an experience, she is a lot closer to that other than she was before the affair."

"You know the thing I often run into," I commented, "is that the woman will say, 'Well, God is up there, but this man with his arms around me is right here.'"

"I know; that's true. Of course, this is why God sent Christ to us, to give us a man with whom we could identify. She will probably say that was two thousand years ago and I have somebody right here who loves me. All I can say in that case is, 'I know exactly how you feel —and yet he is just a man, and you have a whole complex of things to think about. Right now the best thing for you is to look the whole thing over and do what is best for everybody.' In other words, I can offer my genuine concern and tell her I appreciate what it feels like to be in love. It's a great sensation; but still the real world presses down on her, and she must deal with it in the most sensible way she can."

"Suppose now that this Christian woman who is having an affair expresses guilt, but her emotional feelings run so strong that she doesn't want to give him up. How would you deal with the guilt problem?"

"She continues the relationship in spite of her guilt?"

104

I nodded. "Exactly."

"I'd want to know more about the guilty feelings. To try and talk in great detail about them will do her a lot of good, even though there is no real solution at this time. In a way, there is a desensitizing process by bringing it out and looking at the guilt. If her guilt feelings are overwhelming, she needs to realize that there is no sin that God cannot wash away, and that Christ in his ministry was more forgiving of people with their love relationships than he was of many, many other sins. She'd have a lot harder time dealing with her sins of pride, for example. I'd want her to think of Christ as a healer, not one who is putting her in everlasting condemnation. If she wants to wallow around in her guilt and not do anything about her problem, it's important to get her out of that rut—to look at the situation objectively."

"Now, suppose a woman wants to continue the affair and yet she feels guilty about it. She says she can't give up the relationship because she has nothing with which to replace it. Is it best to go along with this for a while, hoping she will gain insight and make the decision herself?"

"As a counselor my role is to help her see the *alternatives*. If she follows this course, then she has to do *this, this, and this*. If she follows that course, then she has to do *that*. Walk down that middle road with her where she makes her decision herself. I think, as a counselor, I can be tremendously helpful if I can toss out a suggestion or prognostication that later on proves to be true, because then she realizes that I am very aware of what is going on."

"Please give me an illustration," I asked.

"Well, she may say to you, 'We've been seeing each other for such and such a length of time and his wife doesn't know anything about it.' I always question that, because in any relationship the wife is going to sense something. So I would answer, 'If he doesn't have that much of a relationship with his wife, what kind of relationship could he have with you? If there is no depth in his marriage, how are you going to have something better?' And she may realize there is a lot more to this than she ever thought! It's refreshing for her to become aware that there is a lot more space to move around in than the narrow, little cubicle in which she has been operating."

"Is it possible to love your own husband again after such an emotional involvement with someone else? A woman will say that she'll never love her husþand as she loved this special man."

"I guess it varies from one person to another. There are women who would say that to their dying day, but what you run into more often is different *qualities* of love. She could resume her marriage in a meaningful, loving way, and yet it wouldn't tap the particular springs of this other relationship. But she can live with that and recognize it. I have known women who have been in love with a man in a way they could never be with their own husbands, and yet they wouldn't want to be married to him because they are so conscious of his problems."

"But doesn't that become a big question mark for a woman? How can she love this other person so deeply and emotionally, and yet remain in her marriage with less feeling?"

"That kind of thing hits in the initial stages, but with time she can become more objective and make the decision to remain in the marriage. When she goes back home to the responsibilities with the children, she may look at the man she's married to and he's really not such a bad guy. A fair number of women just work this out themselves. Their own common sense tells them."

"But what adds fuel to the flame is the sexual experience, which may be so great with this lover and so lacking in the marriage. That colors this whole thing, doesn't it?"

"Yes," he replied thoughtfully, "although I think if she's fifty or over she would say, 'Oh, well . . .' If she's twenty she'd kick out her husband so fast it wouldn't be funny."

"O.K., at twenty and fifty. What about right in between, at thirty-five, and there are children?"

"That's a rough situation. She has probably made the rounds of doctors and finally told somebody that she can't be satisfied sexually in her marriage. First she's looking at other men and having all kinds of fantasies, then she meets a man and is fulfilled sexually—that's terribly strong. However, if she finds her way into my office there is a real investment in her marriage, and I would want to spend some time with her husband and find out why they couldn't make their sex life more satisfying. And that might open up a lot of other things if they really want help."

"Now, what if the woman says to you that she never really had deep love feelings for her husband in the first place? She married him because all her friends were getting married and he seemed to be a nice person, more like a brother, but she never really loved him?"

"If that's true," commented Dr. Mebane, "my first

reaction would be one of disbelief. Only if she repeated those same words on several occasions to me would I believe her. It's so easy to get caught up in a web and say such things, and yet, as she reflects, the facts of the marriage may be otherwise. In counseling you constantly revise viewpoints!"

"I'd like to ask you now whether a wife should confess her infidelity to her husband."

"That's a crucial issue. There are times when a wife's confession would be an utter disaster for a marriage, and there are other times when it would make a lot of sense to tell a husband. She may want you to make that decision for her, but you can't. Frankly, this question makes me terribly uneasy. For one thing, as counselors we don't like the idea of secrets, of being less than honest. Our whole thrust is toward opening things up; and yet I have seen too many instances where this knowledge has been a club with which the other person has beaten his wife or himself. Just a mess. You need to go over all the pros and cons with her. You need to know more about the husband. Would he brood over it? Could he accept it?"

"Do you think it's generally true that a husband finds it more difficult to forgive his wife than she does him?"

"I've seen it both ways. I really don't know. Suppose the husband comes in and confesses that he's had a few affairs and she knows about them. He says, 'I've thought how I would feel if she had an affair. It would really rock me, but I guess I could take it. I'm not perfect.' Then I think it would be good to get it into the open. I wouldn't guarantee there wouldn't be any fireworks, but he'd probably accept it. There are other times when the loving thing to do is to keep your mouth shut."

"How can a person reconcile this emotional involvement with the Christian faith?"

"This relationship in which a woman is caught up triggers emotional responses deep within her being of which she has never been aware. She needs to recognize there is an inner source of energy. The Lord created us as we are; we are not whole and we find our completion in him. Through all our life we will struggle with our imperfections. Emotions, along with our nature, are God given. Our problem is to use our emotions properly in harmony with God's will, his loving will. What is happening to a person in love is a discovery of the power and depth of the emotions. It's not the emotions that are wrong but what we *do* about them! I would therefore open it up to more inquiry, rather than shutting it off with, 'But you must not feel that way.' "

"How would you counsel a person to end the affair?"

"The ideal way would be to have a brief meeting and agree never to see each other again, but that rarely happens. It depends so much on the individual, how it got started, who is putting the major amount of energy into keeping the relationship going, how deep-seated the hang-ups are, how great the dependency is, how manipulative each one is—so many things."

"Suppose this person is working for or with the man she loves at the same place of work. Would you suggest a change of jobs?"

"Well, I might suggest it, but until she comes up with the idea herself it isn't going to get very far. You know, often an affair is over for months before it's over! This state of objectivity has begun to move in and she can look at the man critically. The wild feelings of intense love have subsided. Perhaps she may go on seeing him because of his need, not hers. Now, I know that this woman is getting control of herself, and she may work it out in an easier way for everybody concerned. But if a woman keeps putting herself back into working day after day and going through all kinds of feelings of hell, she is just perpetuating a bad situation. As a counselor I have to say, 'Look, is this the way to treat yourself? Is this the best arrangement you can work out?' This whole business of counseling is really a matter of introducing new ideas, since most of us tend only to see two possibilities, all or none, either-or. There are other options, other alternative ways."

"What steps would you suggest to a woman who wants to renew her marriage?"

"I like to get a couple to talk about how they first met each other, to push them back into an awareness of what it was like back in those days. If they reflect on it, their whole mood changes, their facial expressions change, and they begin to look on their relationship in a way they may not have seen it for years."

"This is my last question," I said. "How can you prevent a reoccurrence?"

"This is where people must become honest with themselves and ask: 'What went wrong? What brought this about in the first place?' A woman needs to look at herself. I think women generally tend to be very objective. If the husband is involved in counseling also, he has to discover what input there has been from his side in these troubles. Lots of counseling with both parties. A crisis can strengthen a marriage, but unless there is quite a bit of housecleaning there will still be a lot of vulnerability. Marriage can be very restrictive to both parties! This is why marriage is in trouble in our day—we haven't freed our partners to be their unique selves. It is a rare marriage where two people really feel free to expand their horizons and, we would hope, bring back into the marriage the things that are really enriching them."

I turned off the tape recorder, and we visited longer before I returned to the airport.

5

From Conflict to Resolution:
Finding the Way

HOW DO YOU OVERCOME an emotional involvement? The
actual resolving of a conflict must be the work of each
individual. No one can do it for you. A counselor may
listen creatively and lovingly, ask some questions that
will loosen up some hidden feelings which are probably
jammed in tight like pickles in a jar, offer you alternatives and insights to help you understand those hidden
forces which create your problems, but not until you
begin to look at yourself realistically will you be able to
make your choices wisely.

The Art of Understanding Yourself

We humans have a habit of looking all around us
for causes, rather than pursuing the more painful process
of probing within. We see a deteriorating marriage, a
pattern of nagging and fighting, a difficult child who
brings out the worst in us, an unmanageable teenager
whose behavior is obnoxious, a living situation which
depresses us because of the neighborhood or the society,
friends basking in an open life-style who have over-
thrown traditional conventions in a newly found freedom, in-laws who fail to be considerate and keep making

unreasonable demands, idealistic dreams that have been smashed by the hard realities of living—any of a number of reasons may lead you to escape and become involved in an affair. And you may reason that these causes (whatever they are in your situation) are to blame without ever searching deeper.

To be sure, there are *always* contributing factors, but they are like little streams that flow into a great river whose waters are already rushing ever downward. Of course life is difficult. Of course there are disappointments. Of course dreams will be shattered. Nevertheless, the basic reasons why you run away from your depressing situation are within you. The stresses of life bearing down upon you may become too great, but that's not the straw that breaks the camel's back. It's the camel's back which is breakable! Of course you can carry too heavy a load, and you need the wisdom to lighten that load. But the art of understanding yourself lies in examining the camel (you). There will always be loads for us to carry.

Unless you understand yourself, you may proceed to break up a marriage (perhaps two marriages), and you are likely to repeat some of the same mistakes. Wherever you go, you take yourself with you on this journey through life.

A woman who had been caught up in more than one affair and was unhappy in her second marriage had this to say about herself: "I have chosen men I've been attracted to but later discovered I really did not like much, nor have these men met my basic needs. The first man I related to was uncommunicative, not affectionate or interested in what I did, and unnaturally secretive." (She referred to a member of her family who had repeatedly involved her in sexual activity from the time she was eight or nine.) "Deep down I wanted to trust this man, but I couldn't. Perhaps I later chose this same type because, regardless of the awfulness of our relationship, it was the only close relationship with a male I had experienced. I also felt I was inferior, since I had been dehumanized by him. Perhaps I thought that I did not *deserve* anything better, and so I have made rash, emotional but wrong choices all my life."

By making these connections in her mind, she was able to understand herself more. She was now free to work at her still faltering marriage.

Most women want to be loved and accepted, to be wanted, to belong, to feel secure. These feelings are more important to them than sexual expression, even though the sexual is for many a beautiful, even necessary, part of the reality of love. But it is *the reality of love,* knowing that she is cherished, knowing that someone really cares, that is essential. When love is absent in a marriage, it is possible to say that the most critical area of a woman's life is slipping out of her control.

The physical union should never be needed to prove love, for when it becomes a matter of proof, love cannot be very solid. Besides, sex alone cannot actually prove anything! Whenever anyone submits too quickly, the other person will wonder about the depth of his or her commitment. Sexual looseness may indicate an escape from one's own loneliness, a compensation for repression, or a need for dominance. It may be merely an attempt to bring some life into the midst of humdrum meaninglessness. But none of that can be called love. It falls far short of the mark. When sex as such becomes a substitute for a deeper relationship, that should raise a thousand questions in your mind. . . .

Why did I get caught in this affair? Do I use people for my gratification? Why do I use people, or why do I allow people to use me? Why did I let myself become attracted? Why am I willing to continue in this relationship? What are my basic needs? What am I trying to find, to prove, to reach, to be? Is there a "spiritual vacuum" within me that seeks fulfillment? Am I really looking for meaning, a reason for being?

"I realize now why I did these things. I needed an alternative!" one woman said frankly. "I've always needed an alternative, even though it was complicating my life. I never could count on *anyone* in my childhood and early adult life, and therefore I've needed to have something else to turn to. Maybe it's a lack of feeling self-sufficient; I suppose so. I don't need those alternatives any longer now. I realize that it just complicates things, but maybe I wanted that too—to complicate things on purpose!"

How can you proceed unless you begin to understand yourself?

Face the Issue

Her letter had a desperate feel to it:

I have a problem that has plagued and disturbed me for quite some time. I have always considered myself to be a religious person. I am an active worker in my church and I enjoy doing this work. I don't feel that I'm self-righteous and have no faults. I just believe in God and Jesus Christ his son. I believe that Christ loves me and has accepted me, and I have always felt, even though despairing at times, that I love Christ.

I am a divorcée who lives alone with my twelve-year-old son. I am presently working on my master's degree. I have been seeing a married man for over three years. He has three children. I care a lot for him, but the situation is getting to me. He has told me not to worry because we would get together one of these days. My problem is that I have been very depressed. Sometimes when I try to pray I seem to be just uttering empty words. I cry a lot. I feel guilt because negative thoughts seem to be ever present when I'm trying to think positively. Many times I feel that these thoughts have made me evil and nobody really cares about me.

When I think of Christ, thoughts seem to crowd in and say I don't care, or why should he care, or even curse words. I immediately ask forgiveness, but I have to force myself back to reality. I've been told that I'm attractive, but I have no real feelings of self-worth. I want God always to be my father. Please help me.

The continuing affair with a married man has become for this divorcée a signal that something is amiss. Her unresolved conflicts are forcing her to raise questions even about her sanity and her destiny. To turn that around—the married man in this case acts like a trigger for her self-awareness, to impel her to examine the crucial issues. Something is being shaken loose within her. The pickles are coming out of the jar one by one, and as the process continues she'll be able to see more clearly who she is and what she really wants out of life. From her letter it appears that she desires God above all, but in the meantime she is depressed and miserable while her inner conflicts cry out for resolution. The resolving of those issues now draws near.

Often an affair is *the pursuit of an illusion,* a dream that we want to press into reality. Illusion is like knocking on a door which has no handle. There is not even a keyhole, and the door refuses to open. Illusion is, in fact, not a door but a wall.

The illusion itself looms like a floating balloon of happiness, with the promise of more and more pleasure. "This was a pleasurable thing, and I can't say even today that it wasn't! It was very warm, very kind, very affectionate, very meaningful, very loving. It was all very lovely, but it is not reality," confesses one of the women in these pages. But Dr. Paul Tournier pricks our balloons:

It is not with toys that we become adult. . . . Instead of resolving problems raised by their dissatisfactions with life, [children] console themselves with trifling pleasures. Viewed in this light, adultery is seen to be a childish act . . . an infantile regression; on the one hand because it is a flight from the responsibilities of this commitment [marriage], and on the other because it means treating someone as a plaything. . . . With his wife [a husband] must face the difficulties of mutual adaptation, of the problems of life, of worries over money or the children's education—in short a dialogue. With the woman he is making love to he has the illusion of a dialogue. . . . He likes to tell her of all his troubles as a child does to his mother.*

It is often difficult to leave our fantasies, to turn our back on some comforting, pleasurable experience and pursue what is after all the hard world we live in. And yet what choices do we have? Do we actually *want* the pain, the heartache, the conflict, and the depressive state of mind that living in a fantasy world inevitably brings us? In some respects we are still able to choose between illusion and reality.

Another far more subtle reason for an affair may be *a self-destructive wish*. And that is a hard fact to accept. But what else is there for a woman who (deliberately) becomes entangled with a married man? Nothing will result from it, unless she forces the issue, and she may not want to live with *that* on her conscience for the rest of her life. So she is quite aware of the dead-end road she travels.

"I wanted to get involved with someone I couldn't have. That would result in another put-down," a woman admitted. She felt so little self-worth that she needed to punish herself. Such a person may accept in theory that God forgives her, but she will not forgive herself. She continues on her self-destructive path, wondering how to reconcile these two opposing life-styles. How can she love another married man and yet believe in God's continuing acceptance of her? This very contradiction

* Dr. Paul Tournier, *The Meaning of Persons* (New York: Harper and Row, 1957), pp. 211–12.

reinforces her need to be chastised. And where did that originate? What influences damaged her early in life so that she now demands this excessive recrimination for herself? Did Christ actually teach us that God wants to condemn us? Certainly not! Then why does she persist on this self-destructive path when Jesus speaks of an abundant, new life? Search for the motivations that keep you in that tangled web!

In this connection we have not yet touched on the side effects of an affair—*the lies and deception* that accompany the cover-up. At home you begin to camouflage your activities and you lie about your whereabouts. Only you know how much you're hiding behind that mask, but you can't talk to anyone about that. You encourage your children to tell the truth—while you're living a lie. You want other people to trust you—while you have become untrustworthy. "I had to lie here and there to cover up. I didn't like that part of me either," confessed one woman.

In so many ways an affair turns into a compromising situation. You're not living up to what you set for yourself as goals, as ideals. Perhaps these ideals were unrealistic in the first place, but they were *your* goals nevertheless. So the battle with integrity is on. Truth in the inward parts? That's a laugh! You are not on the inside what you project on the outside, even while you profess honesty to your lover. You battle your own weaknesses in silence, and you keep on wondering why you're so prone to temptation. You may make resolutions and have times of good intentions, but it's so easy to pick up the phone and start all over again. Living up to what you believe? You may as well throw that ideal out with the trash. And so a deterioration process sets in, a concession with your inner self that eats away at the core like termites destroying what can never be restored.

In spite of all these complications you don't allow yourself to consider where this troublesome adventure will end. You want to face the issue, and yet you have the tendency to avoid decisions. It's not that you're an indecisive person; it's just that, as one wife told me when I asked her where all of this would end for her: "When you are involved like this, that's the *last* thing you think about. You are so engrossed that you always hope that some circumstances will make this relationship permanent." But "miracles" like that rarely if ever occur. So you hold on for years until that final, bitter disappointment. You knew that the relationship was impossible in the first place, that it contained only paper promises—so why were you willing to allow yourself to float downstream that far?

"I learned one thing," one woman confessed after she pulled out of an affair that had lasted almost three years, "I'm very susceptible. I keep my distance with men. I will not allow myself to get too close. At least, that's the way it has to be for me."

The Need for Confession

In order to heal the inner self, our need is for God and not for more guilt. There is already far too much guilt and turmoil and frustration because of our unresolved problems. All that pressure must be relieved. When you have awakened to things as they really are so that you're facing your true self, you need to dump the guilt and, like trash taken out of the house, leave it on the curb to be removed. It will be.

A Christian counselor will hear your confession and pronounce the word of forgiveness. He can't make you forgive yourself, but in the name of the Lord he can assure you that you are forgiven. God alone can effect the healing of the whole person, the bringing together of what has torn you apart. In the final analysis it is to God that we have to come, especially if we are Christians who believe in him.

The real issue at stake is that Christians, while professing to respect and honor God, by adverse actions (such as an affair) actually contradict his will for their lives. It is like an open attack on one of the Ten Commandments, if not on more than one—to commit adultery, to covet someone else's mate, and to put other gods before the only true God. "My chief temptation," a wife admitted, "is to idolize him, to love him more than God." So it is God with whom we deal and God alone who can forgive and restore us.

Augustine defined sin as "a free act of the will whereby we refuse to obey God and turn to ourselves." When we are unaware of the dynamics of selfishness, we may actually become very angry with God. Since we have deliberately broken his laws we feel estranged from him. I asked one wife how she managed to overcome her anger and she replied:

"It came in time, but it took a long time. I still have moments of anger, but what happened months after the affair was that I lost my anger against God and gained back my guilt! It seemed that the less angry I was with God, the more guilty I became about what I had done. Sometimes I still wonder if God punishes me for this affair, but then I have to tell myself that God is not like that."

Interesting! She was angry with God because she wanted to be free to do what she wanted, but when she stopped doing her own will her anger left and guilt set in. She had successfully ignored God for a while, but when she took him seriously again her guilt returned. How else can guilt be removed except through forgiveness? And forgiveness is granted when we, like the prodigal, return from the far country. Through confession we experience God's acceptance and love: *If we freely admit that we have sinned, we find God utterly reliable and straightforward—He forgives our sins and makes us thoroughly clean from all that is evil* (I John 1:9, Phillips).

But now a crucial question arises, one that Dr. Mebane answered briefly in the previous chapter. Should you or should you not confess to your mate? There can be no single answer to that question. It depends entirely upon the individuals. In one case confession could produce disaster. The person "sinned against" may be so devastated that he becomes bitter, resentful, unforgiving, depressed—attitudes which could remain to spread poison throughout the marriage. And eventually it could end in divorce.

On the other hand confession could produce a new openness and honesty, bringing a husband and wife closer together through the mutual bond of sincere forgiveness. Such a confession may finally open the eyes of both partners to other factors which caused this disruption. They may both have wondered what was wrong with their communication. Unfaithfulness, after all, was the symptom of a greater problem. Now they may begin to work together on the total marriage, so a new, healing love can grow out of this crisis.

Should you tell your mate? Well, what type of person is he or she? Would he or she be destroyed by such a confession? The important point is that you confess your sins to God and possibly to another Christian who in the name of Christ can speak the word of forgiveness to you.

Is it possible that your need to confess is a means of placing the burden on the other? It relieves you, of course, but your mate may not be able to carry that burden. No one except Christ can carry your guilt for you (and he already has). Is the motive to confess to your partner a desire to inflict pain? If you believe that he or she was responsible for your fall (was dictatorial, unloving, undemonstrative, critical, antagonistic, stingy, or had other faults), then you may want to get even by telling him all about your transgression. Why was he or she not more understanding and communicative? Your mate could have kept you from straying in the first place! As suicide is often a desperate form of revenge on someone else, so confession could become an unconscious means of revenging ourselves also.

But by now we have learned that no one else is completely responsible for our actions anyway, nor can "they" make us stray. Wanting our own freedom is our will to power—a form of pride—a desire to have our own way rather than do God's will. The root causes are within ourselves. The camel's back is not only broken by the heavy load, but the camel's back is breakable.

We are responsible persons who cannot lay all the blame on circumstances or on the people around us. And that leads us to honest confession before God, and therefore the experience of his renewing forgiveness.

Forgiveness

The secrets which will be shouted from the house-tops are unconfessed secrets. What God has forgiven will not be brought up again. He even forgets our confessed sins. *I will forgive their iniquity, and I will remember their sin no more* (Jeremiah 31:34). And that means that they are removed from the conscious mind of God.

There is great comfort in knowing that all of us have been touched by the sinfulness of mankind, *that every excuse may die on the lips of him who makes it and no living man may think himself beyond the judgment of God. . . . indeed it is the straight-edge of the Law that shows us how crooked we are* (Romans 3:19, 20, Phillips). We may designate the Scripture that *all have sinned* (Romans 3:23) to our pre-Christian days, but it speaks to the general condition of all men. Although Christians are sinners "saved by grace," they remain sinners who are not only capable of falling short of God's glory, but who hardly measure up to perfection.

When John Donne says, "I am still in a slippery state," he reveals a great sensitivity and ends a sermon on Christ's coming to redeem us with these words: "This is the conclusion for every humble Christian: No man is a greater sinner than I was, and I am not sure but that I may fall to be worse than ever I was, except

I . . . employ the talents of God's graces better than I have done." *

Our hope lies in the assurance that we can come back to God again and again and again. If we would be rejected for not living up to the standards God has established for Christians, then none of us would ever make it. But if, as his children, we are allowed to fail and return, then our deepest feelings of rejection will be overcome! This does not mean we should perpetuate wrong. It is dangerous to continue in an adulterous relationship, since our conscience can be quieted and we will try to convince ourselves that everything is all right anyway. We aren't the only ones living like that. But if we truly love God we will not play around with his love as if it had no value.

One woman told me, "I have always realized my dependence upon God, and when I was able to let go of my fantasy world there was room again for God in my life." It's hard to relinquish our strong desires, but when we yield we will not drop into a void. God will receive us.

On the other hand, I can also understand those who have called a halt to their inner struggles and have perpetuated an affair. They have compromised so much already that they believe there is a point of no return. It is easy to give up on yourself, especially when you believe that you have lost your integrity and there is no way back. It's like being expelled from the garden of Eden.

* From the Sermons of John Donne, *The Showing Forth of Christ*, Edmund Fuller, ed. (New York, Harper and Row, 1964), p. 124.

In that connection I am intrigued by the meaning of Paul's simple statement: *Though sin is shown to be wide and deep, thank God His grace is wider and deeper still* (Romans 5:20, Phillips). That means that, no matter how great and perpetual our sins are, the power of God's forgiving love is greater. Sin can always be covered by grace! According to Jesus *every* kind of transgression can be forgiven, except that continual and persistent rejection of the divine offer of pardon, witnessed to us by the Holy Spirit. As much as sin deserves to be punished and does not even dare to hope for relief, so much more is God's mercy offered—with no strings attached. That is true because of the cross of Jesus—he took our sin, our punishment, our judgment, and died in our place. If there is more grace than sin, then no one need despair!

It is important in thinking about forgiveness to grasp the nature of God. God is not only the judge of the world but also the savior. God does not only demand but also forgives. God is not only the holy almighty one but also our compassionate father. He reveals himself (even in the Old Testament) like this: *Let them boast in this alone: That they truly know Me and understand that I am the Lord of justice and of righteousness whose love is steadfast; and that I love to be this way* (Jeremiah 9:24, Living Bible). Ponder that final statement—*I love to be this way!*

Faith and the Will

Having tried to understand ourselves and face the issues, having confessed, and believing in the forgive-

ness of sin, the question now presses hard upon us—
"How do I change myself? How can I come to grips
with these strong inner needs, these urges, these desires?
And, if I want to do the right thing, how do I get the
strength to do it?"

There are Christians who will answer that we live
by faith (and the word of God and prayer and the Holy
Spirit and Christian fellowship and so on). This life
of faith is the result of being born again, and we receive
a new dynamic. Jesus said again and again to those who
came to him for healing that their faith would make
them whole. Through faith you turn to the living Lord
and out of respect for God you do his will. Your emotions are then rechanneled and you should travel down
the narrow way. The presence of the Holy Spirit is given
to every believer in Christ, and by the power of Christ
you will reach the ultimate goal of redemption—the
redemption of the whole person. In short, you live by
faith.

Others insist that you also need to exercise willpower. Unless you want to do the right thing you will
never succeed in overcoming the flesh. You may have
faith and pray a lot, but if you will not think positively
and determine to do God's will, you will fail miserably.
Here the emphasis, although it does not slight faith, is
on willpower—and here I want to make a crucial point
to help us over our predicament.

When Christianity declares that man is imperfect
this means that the *total* man is imperfect. No part of
him is all right. Not only does the flesh induce us to
sin, but the imagination draws pictures, the mind offers
arguments on behalf of the wrong as the will leads us

straight into it! The sexual part is bound up in that weakness, too, and once the choice has been made, that's it. Isn't that obvious from our experience? We *consent* to sin, and the consent is given by our chief enemy—our own will.

My own behaviour baffles me. For I find myself not doing what I really want to do but doing what I really loathe. . . . I often find that I have the will to do good, but not the power. That is, I don't accomplish the good I set out to do, and the evil I don't really want to do I find I am always doing. . . . My conscious mind wholeheartedly endorses the Law, yet I observe an entirely different principle at work in my nature. This is in continual conflict with my conscious attitude, and makes me an unwilling prisoner to the law of sin and death. In my mind I am God's willing servant, but in my own nature I am bound fast. . . . It is an agonising situation, and who on earth can set me free from the clutches of my own sinful nature? I thank God there is a way out through Jesus Christ our Lord. (From Romans 7:15–24, Phillips)

It now follows that moral appeals to the will fall like parental advice on a rebellious teenager. Worse than that—like trying to raise the dead to life. The commands of God which are often contrary to my natural inclinations fail to secure my obedience. What I discover in myself is not that I am so weak, but that I am powerless to will that which is good. In reality I do not exert my will at all. I do not will *sufficiently*, because my will and not only my sexuality is part of that imperfect, fallen self. If I could just bring myself to will, I would be all right. But I don't *want* to do that. My reason is beaten before it even takes the field, and my will is like a pinch hitter who strikes out with the bases loaded.

Does this help to explain why a Christian can fall into sexual sin? The Christian woman involved with a married man may question why the Holy Spirit has not kept her from this entanglement. Is she now again living in the flesh? Does she no longer have the Spirit? Is she lost? But to say that she is lost leads to further confusion, since she still believes in Christ as Lord and savior. Now, who is a perfect Christian? Who does not in one way or another fall every day?

You may believe that if you had a stronger will you would not have yielded to temptation, but that is where you are wrong! The will is damaged too. Or you may reason that if you had more faith you wouldn't have become involved with a married man. Wrong again, because faith alone cannot do it. Faith means far more than just believing in Christianity. Martin Luther put it this way: "Faith is a great art and doctrine which no saint has fathomed fully unless he has found himself in despair, in the anguish of death or in extreme peril."

Only when we have come to the very end of ourselves will we begin to have real faith, and then we become open to God's influence on our lives. In the extremity of despair faith is born. Only that kind of faith can move the heart and marshal the will to overcome. "This kind of faith can only be acquired through a very deep trial," admitted a woman who was shocked by a terrible experience.

My will alone has little power, but by the reality of faith my will is strengthened. That faith is in the living, loving God, so it would be truer to say that by faith *God* strengthens my will. When I believe that he loves and accepts me, I will be motivated in a different way. When I become completely convinced of what God wants for me—but this is the key, I need to be inwardly convinced—then I ask that he control my will and help me to act in accordance with his revealed word.

The Truth and the Way

There is one other stimulus for resolving an affair and finding the way. Truth is absolute. Truth is truth whether I believe it to be true or not. Truth remains truth whether I experience it or not, whether I feel it or not. So—God exists. God does not exist *because* I feel or experience him.

The truth, the right, the good exist apart from my experience and feelings. Therefore when I feel right about something, or I'm "in love" and behave in a manner contrary to God's law, I am not doing right simply because I feel good. If the right is absolute, then my feelings don't validate or disqualify it.

If God exists, and *if* God has revealed his will to man, and *if* we accept truth as absolute, then it follows that I cannot simply state that whatever I do is right. I must behave in accord with the word of God! The implication of this objective reality is that I cannot just carry on spontaneously the way I *feel*. If I proceed as if life is a cafeteria where I can pick and choose what I like, I am not guided by the truth.

This may sound a bit cold and impersonal, but Christians move beyond laws and absolutes to a person who embodies truth, who comes from God in the flesh as our example, our friend, and our savior. We receive light and power from him who not only upholds the law of God, but who warmly and compassionately demonstrates in his life and death the love of God for fallen, selfish persons.

Prone to failure, weak and helpless, we still press toward the high calling of God in Christ. It's the goal to be reached that matters, not only the process but the end result. Therefore, do not allow your failures to keep you from moving toward that ultimate destination. Out of our confession is born a faith that says "Yes" to God and believes that in return God answers: "Yes, I care very much. Yes, I do forgive you. Yes, I love you."

As one habit can be vanquished by a stronger one, so one love will be overcome by a greater love. When the love of Christ enters our lives because *there is no greater love than this—that a man lays down his life for his friends* (John 15:13, Phillips), we will be moved to love him in return. Our highest joy springs not only from being loved but from loving. We can, in fact, turn the same energies which we poured into a human relationship toward our love for God! Are we not to love him with our whole being, heart, soul, and mind? And who is sufficient for that?

The saints have found that their love for God overshadowed all lesser loves. In God lies our hope since it is true that "we are shaped and fashioned by what we love." *

As I have worked over this closing chapter for weeks, reading and revising it, I still sense there is something lacking. It is that indefinable something which actually

* Goethe.

helps a person to begin to change through counseling—sympathetic understanding, creative listening, identification with the hurts of that individual. It is not by words but by something else—an acceptance, maybe, or is it the ministry of God's Spirit?—that a person gains insight and hope so that the courage to change is reborn.

Of course, in counseling there are also ideas expressed, suggestions made, and Scriptures discussed. But what cannot be conveyed on paper is that compassion, that acceptance—yes, that Christian love which surrounds the words as petals surround the life-giving pollen. Transformation will not take place because of words alone—even this last chapter—but because of words and *concern*.

Isn't this true of our Christian experience? When you come to know God, it is not because God speaks beautiful words or gives heavenly advice, but because you are overwhelmed by the action of God, the deeds of salvation, especially by the cross of Christ. You are born anew not by words alone but by the Spirit of God.